FEDERAL OCEANOGRAPHIC FLEET

STATUS REPORT

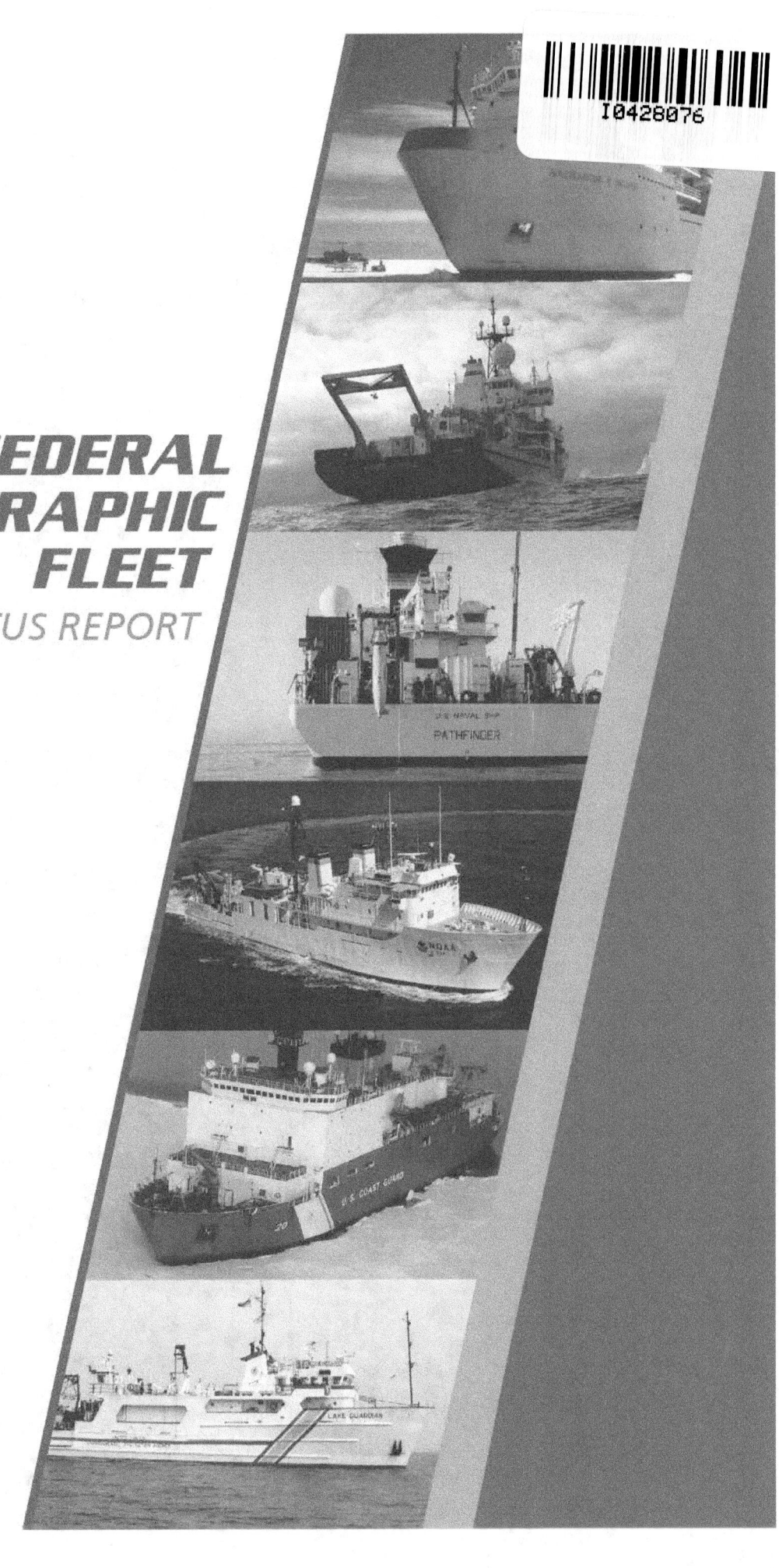

TABLE OF CONTENTS

EXECUTIVE SUMMARY 1

1. INTRODUCTION 3

2. THE FEDERAL OCEANOGRAPHIC FLEET 7
   A. FLEET COORDINATION 7
   B. RESEARCH AND SURVEY SHIPS 9
   C. SHIPS BY CLASS 11

3. FLEET MISSIONS AND UTILIZATION 13
   A. MISSIONS 13
   B. UTILIZATION 17
   C. CHALLENGES AND IMPACTS 20

4. FLEET RENEWAL AND MODERNIZATION 22
   A. 2012–2035: RESEARCH SHIPS 22
   B. 2012–2035: SURVEY SHIPS 26

5. PLANNING CONSIDERATIONS 28
   A. LIFE CYCLE COSTS: PLANNING CONSIDERATIONS, DESIGN,
      ACQUISITION, MAINTENANCE, AND DISPOSAL 28
   B. TECHNOLOGY INFUSION 29
   C. OTHER OPPORTUNITIES 31
   D. POLAR 32
   E. GREEN INITIATIVES 33

6. VISION—THE FUTURE FEDERAL OCEANOGRAPHIC FLEET 35

7. CONCLUSIONS 38

8. REFERENCES 39

APPENDIX 1. SHIPS IN THE FEDERAL OCEANOGRAPHIC FLEET >130 FEET . . . 40

APPENDIX 2. RESEARCH AND SURVEY ACTIVITIES BY AGENCY 41

APPENDIX 3. ACRONYMS AND ABBREVIATIONS 42

May 24, 2013

Dear Colleague:

We are pleased to deliver the enclosed *Federal Oceanographic Fleet Status Report* an inventory of the Nation's fleet of oceanographic-survey and research vessels which updates the last such report, published in 2007. This Fleet Report reviews existing fleet infrastructure and modernization plans to support Federal agency oceanographic operations, surveys, and research; provide access to the world's oceans and Great Lakes; enable data collection, surveys, and scientific ocean research; and support implementation of the National Ocean Policy.

The report finds that, although there has been an increase in the use of satellites, floats, gliders, and other advanced technologies for ocean observation, ships continue to be critical components of the Nation's infrastructure for ocean research and surveys. It concludes, moreover, that strengthened interagency coordination in scheduling, operating, and designing the fleet has already improved efficiency by speeding ship-to-shore transmission of data; incorporating green technologies into ship design and operations; and integrating diverse perspectives and interagency expertise into ship design and operations.

The Fleet Report directly supports the advancement of fundamental science and information objectives set forth in both the *National Ocean Policy Implementation Plan* and the National Science and Technology Council's recently released report, *Science for an Ocean Nation: Update of the Ocean Research Priorities Plan*. It draws on the contributions of the National Ocean Council's member agencies as well as the University National Oceanographic Laboratory System (UNOLS).

We look forward to continuing our work with stakeholders in the public, private, and academic communities to ensure that our Nation's Federal fleet continues to support enhanced understanding, protection, and sustainable use of our ocean resources.

Nancy H. Sutley
Chair, Council on Environmental Quality
Co-Chair, National Ocean Council

John P. Holdren
Director, Office of Science and Technology Policy
Co-Chair, National Ocean Council

NATIONAL OCEAN COUNCIL

Council on Environmental Quality – CO-CHAIR
Office of Science and Technology Policy – CO-CHAIR
Assistant to the President for Domestic Policy
Assistant to the President for Homeland Security and Counterterrorism
Assistant to the President for National Security
Assistant to the President for Economic Policy
Assistant to the President for Energy and Climate Change Program
Department of Agriculture
Department of Commerce, National Oceanic and Atmospheric Administration
Department of Defense
Department of Energy
Department of Health and Human Services
Department of Homeland Security
Department of Interior

Department of Justice
Department of Labor
Department of State
Department of Transportation
Director of National Intelligence
Environmental Protection Agency
Federal Energy Regulatory Commission
Joint Chiefs of Staff
National Aeronautics and Space Administration
National Science Foundation
Office of the Vice President
United States Coast Guard
White House Office of Management and Budget

INTERAGENCY WORKING GROUP ON FACILITIES AND INFRASTRUCTURE*

DARPA Advanced Technology Office	Khine Latt
Department of Energy	Jerry Elwood
Environmental Protection Agency	Kennard W. Potts
Bureau of Ocean and Energy Management	Ronald Lai
National Aeronautics and Space Administration	Paula Bontempi
National Oceanic and Atmospheric Administration	RADM Michael S. Devany (Co-Chair)
National Science Foundation (Division of Ocean Sciences)	Bob Houtman
National Science Foundation (Office of Polar Programs)	Timothy McGovern
Oceanographer of the Navy	Robert Winokur (Co-Chair)
Office of Naval Research	Tim Schnoor
State Department	Margaret F. Hayes
United States Army Corps of Engineers	William Birkemeier
United States Coast Guard	Rajiv Khandpur
United States Geological Survey	John Haines

INTERAGENCY WORKING GROUP ON FACILITIES AND INFRASTRUCTURE SUBGROUP FOR FLEET PLAN

Oceanographer of the Navy	Abby Graefe
Oceanographer of the Navy	Kate Segarra
Oceanographer of the Navy	CDR John Caskey
National Oceanic and Atmospheric Administration	CDR Ralph Rogers
National Oceanic and Atmospheric Administration	LTJG Adrienne Hopper
National Science Foundation (Division of Ocean Sciences)	Bob Houtman
National Science Foundation (Office of Polar Programs)	Timothy McGovern
University National Oceanographic Laboratory System	Jon Alberts
United States Coast Guard	Jon Berkson
Environmental Protection Agency	Kennard Potts
Office of Naval Research	Tim Schnoor
United States Geological Survey	John Haines
Bureau of Ocean Energy Management	Ronald Lai
Department of State	Elizabeth Tirpak
National Aeronautics and Space Administration	Paula Bontempi

*The Interagency Working Group on Facilities and Infrastructure (IWG-FI) operates under the Administration's National Ocean Council structure and provides guidance on requirements and other matters relating to National oceanographic assets to its parent body, the Subcommittee on Ocean Science and Technology (SOST).

SUBCOMMITTEE ON OCEAN SCIENCE AND TECHNOLOGY

Arctic Research Commission . . . . John Farrell
Department of Agriculture . . . . Louie Tupas
Department of Commerce, National Oceanic and Atmospheric Administration . . . . . Robert Detrick, Co-Chair; Craig McClean
Department of Defense, U.S. Army Corps of Engineers . . . . Charles Chesnutt
Department of Defense, U.S. Navy . . . . Don Schregardus
Department of Defense, Office of Naval Research . . . . Joan Cleveland
Department of Energy, Office of Science . . . . Gerald Geernaert
Department of Health and Human Services, Centers for Disease Control and Prevention . Lorraine Backer
Department of Health and Human Services, Food and Drug Administration . . . . . . Robert Dickey
Department of Health and Human Services, National Institutes of Health . . . . . . Allen Dearry
Department of Homeland Security, U.S. Coast Guard . . . . Jonathan Berkson
Department of the Interior, BOEM . . . . Rodney Cluck
Department of the Interior, U.S. Geological Survey . . . . John Haines
Department of Justice . . . . Matt Leopold
Department of State . . . . David Balton
Department of Transportation Maritime Administration . . . . Richard Corley
Environmental Protection Agency . . . . Jonathan Garber
Executive Office of the President Council on Environmental Quality . . . . VACANT
Executive Office of the President Domestic Policy Council . . . . VACANT
Executive Office of the President Office of Management and Budget . . . . John ten Hoeve
Executive Office of the President Office of Science and Technology Policy . . . . . Brendan Kelly, Co-Chair
Joint Chiefs of Staff . . . . Robert Winokur
National Aeronautics and Space Administration . . . . Jack Kaye
National Science Foundation . . . . David Conover, Co-Chair
Marine Mammal Commission . . . . Dennis Heinemann
Smithsonian Institution . . . . Leonard Hirsch

EX-OFFICIO MEMBERS

SOST Interagency Working Group on Facilities and Infrastructure (IWG-FI) | Co-Chairs: Robert Winokur, RADM Michael Devany
SOST Interagency Working Group on Harmful Algal Blooms, Hypoxia, and Human Health (IWG-4H) | Co-Chairs: Paul Sandifer, Lorrie Backer
SOST Interagency Working Group on Ocean Acidification (IWG-OA) | Chair: Ned Cyr
SOST Interagency Working Group on Ocean and Coastal Mapping (IWG-OCM) | Co-Chairs: John Brock, Jennifer Wozencraft, Ashley Chappell
SOST/SIMOR Joint Interagency Working Group on Ocean Education (IWG-OE) | Co-Chairs: Lisa Rom, Marlene Kaplan
SOST Interagency Ocean Observations Committee (IOOC) | Co-Chairs: David Legler, Bob Houtman, Eric Lindstrom
SOST Interagency Working Group on Ocean Partnerships (IWG-OP) | Co-Chairs: Rodney Cluck, Craig McLean
SOST Interagency Working Group on Ocean Social Science (IWG-OSS) | Co-Chairs: Marilyn ten Brink, Tom Fish
Ocean Research and Resources Advisory Panel (ORRAP) | Chair: Margaret Leinen
Subcommittee on Oceans Policy of the Global Environment Policy Coordinating Committee (Oceans Sub-PCC) | Chair: David Balton
Ocean Resource Management-Interagency Policy Committee (ORM-IPC) | Co-Chairs: Sally Yozell, Eileen Sobeck, Don Schregardus
SOST Policy Advisors | Lora Clarke, Roxanne Nikolaus

SHIP OWNERS / OPERATORS

NSF

The **National Science Foundation** (NSF) funds research activities that span the globe, from domestic coastal waters to remote polar regions, in support of its mission to promote the progress of science, basic research, and education. NSF's research ships advance programs in biological, chemical, and physical oceanography; marine geology and geophysics; and oceanographic technology development. On behalf of the United States Antarctic Program, NSF leases one research icebreaker and one ice-reinforced research vessel to support science operations in the Antarctic. NSF contracts with the U.S. Coast Guard to provide research icebreaker support for Arctic ocean science operations and is constructing an ice-strengthened research vessel scheduled for delivery in 2013. NSF contracts national and international sources for heavy icebreaking services and also leases a vessel for deep ocean drilling activities. *http://www.nsf.gov*

ONR

The **Navy's Office of Naval Research** (ONR) funds basic and applied research and technology demonstrations in support of near-term and future naval capabilities needed for the preservation of national security. ONR research ships support its programs in coastal geosciences, ocean acoustics, ocean engineering, undersea signal processing, marine meteorology, physical oceanography, and ocean optics, and biology, primarily carried out by university laboratories through funded grants. *http://www.onr.navy.mil*

NAVOCEANO

The **Naval Oceanographic Office** (NAVOCEANO) optimizes seapower by applying relevant oceanographic knowledge in support of U.S. national security. NAVOCEANO conducts multidisciplinary ocean surveys in support of national and Navy requirements, provides global oceanographic and geospatial products and services to meet the Department of Defense and Navy safe navigation and weapon/ sensor performance requirements, and generates and disseminates global oceanographic observations and forecasts to Naval forces. *http://www.navo.navy.mil*

EPA

The **Environmental Protection Agency** (EPA) owns and operates two ships. OSV *Bold* operates in the Atlantic and Pacific Oceans and the Caribbean Sea to monitor water quality, effects of dredged material, coral reef health, and other special assessments. R/V *Lake Guardian* operates in the Great Lakes, monitoring water quality and studying the biological community. *http://www.epa.gov*

NOAA

The **National Ocean and Atmospheric Administration's** (NOAA) mission is centered around science, service, and stewardship.
- To understand and predict changes in climate, weather, ocean, and coasts
- To share that knowledge and information with others
- To conserve and manage coastal and marine ecosystems and resources

Underlying NOAA's continued success is its unique infrastructure. NOAA's core mission functions require satellite systems, ships, buoys, aircraft, research facilities, high-performance computing, and information management and distribution systems. NOAA's fleet of research and survey ships collect hydrographic and coastal assessment data, conduct fisheries scientific survey operations and ocean exploration, and collect sustained oceanographic and atmospheric data in various marine environments. *http://www.noaa.gov*

USCG

The **United States Coast Guard** (USCG) has three fundamental roles: maritime safety, security, and stewardship. To carry out these roles, USCG has 11 missions: ports, waterways, and coastal security; drug interdiction; aids to navigation; search and rescue; living marine resources; marine safety; defense readiness; migrant interdiction; marine environmental protection; ice operations; and other law enforcement. USCG ships are indirectly part of the Federal Fleet. In support of the oceanographic fleet, USCG provides icebreaking services that give NSF and the other Federal agencies access for research in the Arctic. USCG polar icebreakers are also capable of breaking a channel into McMurdo Sound in support of resupply efforts for research facilities in Antarctica. *http://www.uscg.mil*

SHIP USERS

BOEM

On October 1, 2011, the **Bureau of Ocean Energy Management, Regulation and Enforcement** (BOEMRE), formerly the Minerals Management Service, was replaced by the Bureau of Ocean Energy Management (BOEM) and the Bureau of Safety and Environmental Enforcement (BSEE) as part of a major reorganization. BOEM is responsible for managing development of the Nation's offshore resources in an environmentally and economically responsible way. BOEM has a critical mission to protect the environment while ensuring the safe development of the Nation's offshore energy and marine mineral resources. BOEM scientists conduct and oversee research that may use the Federal Oceanographic Fleet to acquire physical, atmospheric, biological, chemical, and geological data in support of safe and environmentally sound exploration; aid in the development and production of offshore natural gas, oil, and marine minerals; manage Outer Continental Shelf renewable energy; and assess environmental impacts and policies, regulations, and procedures to mitigate potential impacts. *http://www.boem.gov*

NASA

The **National Aeronautics and Space Administration** (NASA) mission is to drive advances in science, technology, and exploration to enhance knowledge, education, innovation, economic vitality, and stewardship of the Earth. NASA's vision is to lead scientific and technological advances in aeronautics and space for a Nation on the frontier of discovery. NASA uses satellite and in situ observations and modeling to help answer scientific questions about the ocean and its role in the Earth system and climate. The Federal Oceanographic Fleet is used to support in situ research and applications, calibration of space-based sensors, and validation of remotely sensed data products. *http://www.nasa.gov*

USGS

The **U.S. Geological Survey** (USGS) of the Department of Interior provides scientific information to describe and understand Earth; minimize loss of life and property from natural disasters; manage water, biological, energy, and mineral resources; and enhance and protect our quality of life. USGS uses the Federal Oceanographic Fleet and commercial vessels to characterize, monitor, and assess resource and hazard potential across state and Federal waters and to conduct research on natural and human drivers of environmental change. *http://www.usgs.gov*

Other Agencies involved in ship issues include the **Department of Energy**, the **Defense Advanced Research Projects Agency**, the **U.S. Army Corps of Engineers**, and the **Department of State**.

EXECUTIVE SUMMARY

The Federal Oceanographic Fleet continues to be a critical national infrastructure that supports Federal agency and academic oceanographic operations, surveys, and research across a broad spectrum of national needs. Ships provide access to the world ocean and Great Lakes, and enable data collection and research for thousands of stakeholders from academia, government, and the public. This status report, prepared by the Interagency Working Group on Facilities and Infrastructure (IWG-FI), updates the December 2007 *Federal Oceanographic Fleet Status Report*. As costs continue to escalate, this report serves as a foundation for efficient and effective Fleet operations at the lowest possible life-cycle costs. Improving coordination and efficiency across the Federal government and with non-Federal partners are key principles of the National Ocean Policy (see *http://www.whitehouse.gov/administration/eop/oceans/policy*).

The Fleet is composed of research and survey ships greater than 40 meters (130 feet) in length owned and operated or leased by the government, along with those Federally or institutionally owned ships operated by the member institutions of the University National Oceanographic Laboratory System. The Fleet has four ship classes based primarily on size:

Global Class ships are the largest and most capable with the ability to work worldwide with the greatest endurance and large scientific parties.

Ocean Class ships are slightly smaller than Global Class vessels and are highly capable but typically not globally ranging. This class includes the older and less-capable "Intermediate" ships that are being phased out.

Regional Class ships are smaller than Ocean Class vessels and are optimized for operation in coastal waters, bays, and estuaries.

Local Class ships are the smallest and are used primarily in waters adjacent to their home ports. Most of these ships are not Federally owned and thus are not addressed in this report.

IWG-FI member agencies have moved forward with Fleet modernization and right-sizing (i.e., identifying proper size of Federal Fleet to meet the Nation's mission requirements) activities identified in the 2007 status report with delivery of one Global Class and four Ocean Class ships and the retirement of one Global Class, four Ocean Class, and one Regional Class ships. Coordination among agencies has significantly increased, including: program implementation for the rapid flow of data from ships at sea to land-based National online archives (i.e., Rolling Deck To Repository), incorporation of green technologies into ship design and operations, increased use of shared equipment pools, cross-linkage of ship scheduling processes, and greater participation in developing cross-agency ship construction and design plans.

Modernization efforts will continue from 2013 through 2022 with the planned addition of six vessels and retirement of nine vessels. With the introduction of highly advanced ships and the retirement of older, less-capable vessels, the Fleet will become more efficient and capable of supporting stakeholders' demands over the next decade. Starting in 2022, the Fleet will experience a reduction in size and capacity due to several vessels nearing their projected end of service life. These impacts are being addressed by the IWG-FI based on requirements and available funding.

NOAA

1. INTRODUCTION

The Federal Oceanographic Research and Survey Fleet consists of sophisticated ships that permit scientists to survey and conduct research on the complex ocean, seafloor, and sub-seafloor environment, as well as the most remote polar regions of the world. Ships in the Federal Oceanographic Fleet are instrumental in collecting observational data on Earth systems that provide a foundation for understanding how these systems interact and for improved modeling. Survey vessels play a vital role in providing high-quality data that are used to inform the public and advise natural resource managers. Research vessels are important educational platforms for graduate students and undergraduates in the marine sciences, providing valuable training and at-sea experiences for young researchers. Ships in the Federal Oceanographic Fleet also provide opportunities for teachers to acquire skills that translate into innovative class projects, thereby inspiring a new generation of scientists.

Through at-sea sampling and observing, researchers have begun to understand, model, and predict the responses of marine populations to both long-term and episodic changes in ocean conditions. Scientific ocean drilling and seismic reflection surveys have led to a deeper understanding of Earth's physical state that can generate earthquakes. Data collected by ships have led to the identification of new energy resources and the discovery of life in extreme environments at and below the seafloor, and enable the search for marine organisms with the potential to treat or cure human diseases. Mapping and analyzing ancient ocean sediments have revealed changes in deep ocean circulation and heat distribution around the planet, leading to a better understanding of the causes and consequences of current climate changes.

Long-term data series and recordings of the conditions at and below the ocean's surface have provided information that is critical to agriculture, fishing, and severe weather prediction, and will lead to a better assessment of the natural variability in Earth's climate system.

OCEANOGRAPHIC SHIPS MAKE IT POSSIBLE TO:

- Conduct basic research on the ocean and ocean floor's physical, chemical, geological, and biological processes and interactions.
- Support research and sensor placement that enable disaster warnings to be issued for hurricanes and tsunamis.
- Support biomedical research in the marine realm to enable discovery of new pharmaceuticals and therapies.
- Provide tactical and strategic oceanographic information in support of national defense and homeland security.
- Understand and assess the status of living resources (e.g., fisheries) to provide the best available information for use by quota and allocation resource and conservation managers and policy-makers.
- Map, sample, and monitor physical, biological, geological, and chemical ocean features that influence weather and climate.
- Provide critically important navigational information to support the safe and effective movement of commerce and transportation within U.S. ports.
- Construct Earth's geologic and/or climatic history as recorded in corals, the ocean floor, and polar ice.
- Discover and protect archeological resources to enable studies about how ancient civilizations used the sea.
- Assess ocean resources and renewable energy for sound management and development.
- Enhance ocean science educational programs and inspire teachers as well as the general public.
- Deploy new instruments and technology that extend ocean sensing to other platforms, such as remotely operated vehicles, autonomous underwater vehicles (undersea gliders and propeller-driven), drifters, and profiling floats.

Ships in the Federal Oceanographic Fleet enable fundamental and applied research in coastal regions of the United States, which are among our Nation's most valuable natural resources. Holding more than 50% of the U.S. population on only 17% of the Nation's land area, coastal communities make substantial contributions to economic growth, quality of life, and national security. As users and stewards of coastal regions and of the deep ocean, we need to better understand and predict how the ocean margin environment responds to

environmental perturbations. The Federal Oceanographic Fleet enables scientists, managers, and decision-makers to monitor pollution that causes red tides, fish kills, and other harmful events; assess and enable the sustained use of our Nation's fish stocks; evaluate permit applications for dredging and drilling; protect and restore coastal ecosystems; and improve the safety and security of our Nation's harbors and maritime transportation routes.

The Federal Oceanographic Fleet provides rapid-response support for catastrophic events and natural disasters around the globe. For example, NOAA, NSF, ONR, and University National Oceanographic Laboratory System (UNOLS) vessels played key roles in collecting water, fish, shellfish, and sediment samples in the wake of the Deepwater Horizon oil spill (2010) to determine both human-health risks and impacts to the living marine resources. The Navy survey vessel, USNS *Henson*, was instrumental in mapping coastal bathymetry changes immediately after the Haiti earthquake (2010) to allow for safe navigation, and assisted in recovery operations for a downed civilian aircraft off Bonaire (2009) after a special request was received from the Dutch government. Following Hurricane Irene (2011), a NOAA hydrographic vessel surveyed the Port of Hampton Roads to facilitate the reopening within 72 hours to resume maritime commerce.

A robust Federal fleet of vessels and aircraft is required to conduct monitoring, mapping, enforcement, response, and safety activities in both coastal waters and the open ocean... the Nation will always need to maintain a Federal fleet that can quickly and effectively respond to environmental disasters, conduct assessments on a routine basis, and enforce applicable laws. Regular upgrades to these vessels and aircraft are needed to incorporate cutting-edge technologies, increase fleet capacity, and address both national and international safety requirements.

— *USCOP, 2004*

This *Federal Oceanographic Fleet Status Report* describes the current and planned Fleet capacity and modernization efforts for all Federal oceanographic research and survey ships that are coordinated by the Interagency Working Group on Facilities and Infrastructure (IWG-FI) through a long-standing interagency process. The IWG-FI recognizes the importance of continually assessing and defining both Fleet capacity and the capabilities needed to support agency missions and the National Ocean Policy. A broad range of options will be considered when evaluating the most cost-effective ways to meet the national ocean research infrastructure needs, including interagency collaboration, increased capabilities from new technology solutions, and private-sector resources where appropriate.

Future trends include a fleet composed of both adaptable, general purpose platforms and specialized ships to meet a broad range of research activities; sustaining the number of larger, general purpose platforms; and growing the capabilities and numbers of smaller ships.

— NRC, 2011a

USCG

2. THE FEDERAL OCEANOGRAPHIC FLEET

A. FLEET COORDINATION

The IWG-FI, under the Subcommittee on Ocean Science and Technology (SOST), is the mechanism that Federal agencies use to coordinate Fleet-related issues. These interactions date back to the early 1980s and include discussions about specific agency ship requirements, activities related to the operations of ships currently in the Fleet, as well as near-term plans for the disposition of ships and opportunities for transfer between agencies to fulfill specific mission needs. Agencies share information about ongoing efforts to enhance support through new science tools, opportunities for reducing the environmental impact of ships, and improving access to the sea for the disabled by increasing ships' compliance with the Americans with Disabilities Act. There has been a significant increase in the level of coordination and collaboration through equipment sharing and the establishment of centralized winch, wire, and van pools. A new initiative has also been successful in creating a pool of skilled science support technicians who can be easily assigned throughout the Fleet for augmentation of cruises requiring a greater level of support. An ongoing important topic of discussion is ship scheduling and, in support of the National Ocean Policy, the IWG-FI is actively investigating options for increased coordination among agencies. Already across the Federal Oceanographic Fleet, interested parties can access ships schedules and obtain agency contact information on each agency's individual ship websites. In 2010,

NOAA, ONR, and NSF held several meetings with UNOLS to discuss operations, shared experiences, scheduling concerns, and lessons learned. UNOLS representatives are also active participants in the IWG-FI discussions to ensure all agency members are aware of ongoing activities related to scheduling, operations, technician support, and fleet planning. UNOLS scheduling meetings and teleconferences are open and UNOLS actively enlists input from the other Federal agencies.

Ship acquisition continues to be conducted through agency specific budget requests and associated appropriations. Through the IWG-FI, there is increased coordination as agencies consider decisions to retire older ships and proceed with designs for new ships. For example, NSF has participated in the design reviews for the two Ocean Class research vessels currently under construction by the Navy. The Navy and NSF collaborated on fleet upgrades to over-the-side handling equipment to reduce the number of personnel required on deck during science operations and to further improve safety. NOAA and NSF have discussed possible collaborations and synergies regarding needs to modernize their mid-sized research ships. NOAA is participating in design refresh activities as NSF moves ahead with the Regional Class Research Vessels (RCRV) Project. Possible future approaches include using a common hull design for the RCRV with options for agency-specific mission configurations during the later construction stages. NOAA is also examining the Navy AGOR design as a replacement option for the larger survey class vessels. In addition, USCG has established an Integrated Product Team, inviting representatives from NSF, NOAA, and other agencies to assist with the development of the multi-agency requirements for a new heavy polar icebreaker.

The IWG-FI meets several times per year to coordinate activities and establish task forces, working groups, or subcommittees to further investigate specific areas of interest. The Subcommittee on Unmanned Systems has been chartered to focus on opportunities to increase coordination on unmanned air, surface, and subsurface vehicles (described later).

B. RESEARCH AND SURVEY SHIPS

As of January 1, 2012, there are 47 ships in the Federal Oceanographic Fleet with an overall length greater than 40 m (130 ft) (see Table 1). Of these 47 ships, two are under long-term lease by the Federal government and three are owned by academic institutions. The ships are grouped into Research and Survey categories, based on their primary purpose and capabilities.

RESEARCH SHIPS carry a broad array of scientific instrumentation, winches, wires, cranes, and articulating frames capable of supporting activities such as water-column and seafloor sampling, monitoring, and acoustic and bathymetric mapping. Laboratories equipped with sophisticated analytical equipment and computers allow preliminary data analysis and sample storage while underway. Data collected often provide real-time input into cruise execution, enabling scientists to make adjustments to mapping or sampling

A. Fundis © University of Washington 2011

plans. Most vessels are multipurpose and are able to conduct a variety of research activities during a single expedition. Some research ships are specialized, having the ability to conduct multichannel seismic operations, deploy and recover human-occupied vehicles (HOVs), recover long sediment and rock cores, and conduct ocean drilling experiments in all parts of the ocean, or operate at high latitudes in the Arctic and Antarctic Oceans.

SURVEY SHIPS acquire a wide range of oceanographic, atmospheric, hydrographic, fisheries stock assessment, ecosystem, and habitat data in direct support of resource management and monitoring programs. Survey ships are frequently involved with temporal and spatial studies to monitor, document, and report changing trends. Ship-mounted sensors collect continuous oceanographic and atmospheric data. J-frames, A-frames, cranes, and winches are used to deploy scientific equipment,

Navy.

including trawl nets, longlining gear, small boats, autonomous underwater vehicles (AUVs), and conductivity-temperature-depth (CTD) sensors. Laboratories carry a variety of calibrated instruments for on-site data processing and analysis, specialized software, software suites for nautical chart development and scientific computer systems, and sample storage. The majority of today's survey ships are specially designed to meet specific mission requirements. NOAA's Fisheries Survey Vessels (FSVs) have been acoustically quieted in accordance with standards defined by the International Council for Exploration of the Seas, while others have been equipped to collect high-resolution bathymetry, gravity, and magnetic data to enable construction of detailed seafloor maps.

All vessels in the Federal Oceanographic Fleet are floating laboratories capable of providing at-sea educational experiences. Below are some examples of at-sea programs that enhance public awareness and bring oceanography into the classroom.

Dive and Discover is an interactive distance-learning website designed to immerse viewers in the excitement of discovery and exploration of the deep seafloor. *http://www.divediscover.whoi.edu*

Since 1999, the **Marine Advanced Technology Education (MATE) Center** has been placing college students in at-sea and land-based internships. MATE has placed over 250 students in internships, more than 150 of which were on UNOLS vessels. *http://www.marinetech.org/education/internships/intern_info.php*

By providing an interdisciplinary research experience, NOAA's **Teacher at Sea (TAS) program** enhances teachers' understanding of our ocean planet and how maritime work and studies are conducted, and increases their level of environmental literacy. *http://teacheratsea.noaa.gov*

NOAA's **Ocean Exploration program** strives to enhance environmental literacy by allowing the public to participate in the excitement of ocean discovery along with scientists. Increasing this literacy requires high-quality, effective collaborations between ocean explorers and America's teachers. *http://oceanexplorer.noaa.gov*

NSF's **Polar Teachers and Researchers Exploring and Collaborating (PolarTREC)** is an educational research experience in which K–12 teachers participate in polar research, working closely with scientists as a pathway to improving science education. The Arctic Research Consortium of the United State manages this NSF-funded program. *http://www.polartrec.com*

The Federal agencies have also funded UNOLS cruises that instruct early career scientists on how to be chief scientists.

C. SHIPS BY CLASS

Research and Survey ships are categorized by class based on size. This status report assigns ships in the Fleet to one of four classes (Table 1); however, it addresses only the largest three classes because of their significant modernization, maintenance, and operating costs.

GLOBAL CLASS: With their extensive deck space, equipment, and a broad and diverse complement of laboratory space and outfitting, they are equipped to handle a wide array of instruments and to deploy suites of moorings, autonomous vehicles, large and complex sampling tools, and sophisticated acoustical equipment. Some vessels in this class support specialized services, including the operation of deep-submergence vehicles or multichannel seismic reflection equipment. Some are ice-strengthened (e.g., ship's hull is reinforced with strengthening cross members and double planking) for operations in higher latitudes.

OCEAN/INTERMEDIATE CLASS: Designed to support integrated, interdisciplinary research and survey missions with many of the same capabilities of the modern Global Class. Generally operating from their home port, these ships will occasionally work worldwide. The older and smaller Intermediate vessels of this class are being phased out as they are less capable of meeting the requirements of the scientists.

REGIONAL CLASS: These vessels operate on the continental shelf and in the open ocean of specific geographic regions. Regional Class vessels are designed to optimize unique regional conditions, such as the capability to work in shallower areas like estuaries and bays, or under seasonally harsh weather conditions. Regional Class are the smallest vessels for which Federal funding is anticipated to be the primary source for construction.

Table 1. Ship Classes

Ship Performance / Class	Global	Ocean/ Intermediate	Regional	Local
Number of ships	16	23	6	6
Endurance	50 days	40 days	30 days	20 days
Range	13,500 nm	10,800 nm	8,100 nm	5,400 nm
Length	> 230 ft	180–230 ft	130–180 ft	< 130 ft
Science berths	30–35	20–25	15–20	15 or less

New types of ship designs, such as twin hulls, may lead to vessels having capabilities similar to those of a larger class. Local class and small boats are not addressed in this Fleet Status Report and should not be counted against the 47 ships currently operating in the Federal Oceanographic Fleet.

COASTAL/LOCAL CLASS: These vessels serve a crucial role in supporting science throughout our Nation's coastal zone, where human impacts of development and resource use are greatest. The science missions are largely driven by local and regional needs. For the purposes of this status report, they are not considered since the majority are not Federally owned.

The Federal agencies also have a large complement of smaller boats and water craft that are operated and maintained at geographically dispersed facilities to support oceanographic research and survey missions. The NOAA Small Boat Program manages a collection of over 400 small vessels (under 300 gross tons) that perform various data collection missions for NOAA throughout the United States and its territories. Vessels vary in size from a simple 3 m (10 ft) kayak to a complex 25 m (85 ft) research vessel. The majority of NOAA's small boats operate in nearshore environments, but extended missions in deepwater environments are common among the larger vessels. These vessels perform missions such as hydrographic surveys, fishing, diving, scientific instrument deployment/ recovery, water and air quality monitoring, law enforcement, and marine mammal surveys. In addition, the NSF's Office of Polar Programs maintains a modest fleet of small boats to support research at Palmer Station, Antarctica. These vessels permit extended science operations around Anvers Island and the surrounding Antarctic Peninsula regions. Operations include support of scientific diving, monitoring, and tagging of whales and other marine mammals, and field camp support on other islands.

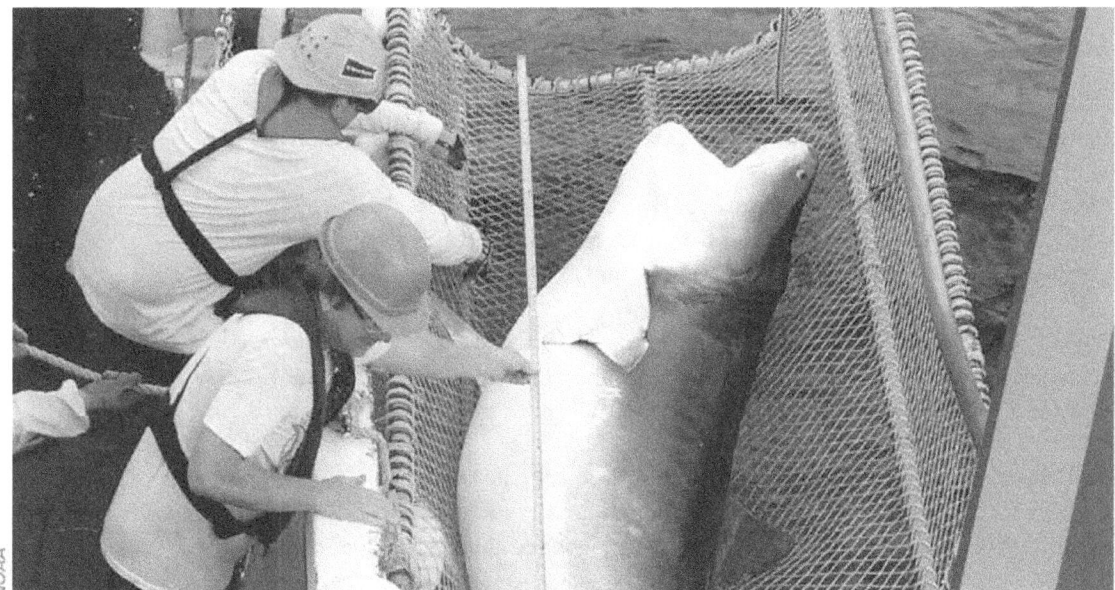

NOAA

3. FLEET MISSIONS AND UTILIZATION

A. MISSIONS

This *Federal Oceanographic Fleet Status Report* highlights the current agency missions supported by the Fleet and identifies future trends based on ocean science assessments. Oceanographers require access to the sea to conduct research and ships will continue to be an essential component of the ocean research infrastructure (USCOP, 2004; NRC, 2009; Augustine et al., 2012). The ships operated by Federal agencies are largely responsible for meeting statutory survey requirements, whereas the academic research fleet is designed primarily to satisfy a wide array of academic research requirements. The *Ocean Research Priorities Plan and Implementation Strategy* (NST Joint Subcommittee on Ocean Science and Technology, 2007) provides additional insight into research areas to be considered important to the national interest.

NOAA's emphasis on *science*, *service*, and *stewardship* focus on four goals: healthy oceans, resilient coastal communities and economies, a weather-ready Nation, and climate adaptation and mitigation. NOAA's fleet plays an integral role in implementing the agency's vision for a healthy society, economy, and environment to support (NOAA, 2010):

- Improved understanding of ecosystems to inform resource management decisions
- Safe, efficient, and environmentally sound marine transportation
- Reduced loss of life, property, and disruption from high-impact events
- Improved scientific understanding of the changing climate system and its impacts

NOAA's multipurpose platforms provide access to a diverse mix of operational systems to meet the statutory requirements mandated through legislation.

Magnuson-Stevens Fishery Conservation and Management Act: Under this act, NOAA manages the fisheries and promotes conservation by rebuilding overfished fisheries, protecting essential fish habitat, and reducing by-catch.

Endangered Species Act: Under this act, NOAA provides for the conservation of species that are endangered or threatened throughout all or a significant portion of their range, and the conservation of the ecosystem on which they depend.

Marine Mammal Protection Act: Under this act, NOAA provides oversight and guidance on the conservation of marine mammals, endangered species, and their habitats in cooperation with regional offices, science centers, and various partners.

Coast and Geodetic Survey Act of 1947: Under this act, NOAA is required to provide nautical charts and products for safe maritime commerce and navigation.

National Marine Sanctuaries Act: Under this act, NOAA is authorized to designate and protect areas of the marine environment with special national significance due to their conservation, recreational, ecological, historical, scientific, cultural, archeological, educational, or esthetic qualities as national marine sanctuaries.

National Environmental Policy Act: Under this act, NOAA is required to integrate environmental values into their decision-making processes by considering the environmental impacts of their proposed actions and reasonable alternatives to those actions.

NOAA continues to upgrade vessel capabilities and is validating its survey requirements to better define long-term recapitalization needs. NOAA will support the integrity of the Federal Oceanographic Fleet and complement the Fleet academic research capabilities with their survey capacity and capabilities.

USCG supports Arctic research missions by operating their polar icebreakers on a reimbursable basis for Federal partners, primarily NSF. In addition, USCG supports NOAA with cutters, boats, and aircraft resource hours that help maintain their National Data Buoy System.

NSF funds research activities that span the globe in support of its mission to promote the progress of science, basic research, and education. NSF's research ships advance science programs in biological, chemical, and physical oceanography;

marine geology and geophysics; and oceanographic technology development. NSF funds a large percentage of the work conducted from the Federal Oceanographic Fleet research ships.

NSF will continue to support basic and applied research and therefore it is anticipated that infrastructure support will also be needed. Increased focus on climate change, ocean circulation, and environmental and fisheries research in the seasonally ice-covered waters in the Alaskan region is driving the need for a more capable, ice-strengthened vessel to operate in this harsh environment. R/V *Sikuliaq*, a Global Class ice-capable research vessel, is projected to be ready for unrestricted science operations in 2014.

The NSF Office of Polar Programs (OPP) supports fundamental research, including climate-change studies in the Arctic Ocean and in the waters surrounding Antarctica. Platforms, including leased ice-capable research vessels, internationally owned heavy icebreakers, ice-reinforced fuel tankers, and cargo ships from the Military Sealift Command provide support for the United States Antarctic Program (USAP) and other high-latitude research activities.

In addition, the academic science community has demonstrated the value of an advanced-technology ocean drillship that can return the highest-quality seafloor sediment, fluid, and rock samples to conduct research on environmental change, processes, and effects; solid Earth cycles and geodynamics; and the deep biosphere. Drilling activities by the Integrated Ocean Drilling Program (IODP) are projected to continue and improved ship capabilities should enable increased scientific productivity.

NAVOCEANO has technical control of six multi-purpose oceanographic survey ships. These vessels are designed and constructed to provide the full spectrum of oceanographic capabilities in coastal and deep-ocean areas. Surveyors onboard collect multidisciplinary global oceanographic, hydrographic, and geophysical data used to gain a better understanding of the ocean's volumetric physical oceanography and seabed properties. This data is used to support the warfighter, navigational safety, and the Navy's Undersea Warfare and Maritime Homeland Defense activities.

Typical missions of NAVOCEANO vessels may include oceanographic sampling and data collection of surface water, mid-water, and ocean floor parameters; launch and recovery of small boats known as hydrographic survey launches; launch, recovery, and towing of scientific packages (both tethered and autonomous), including handling, monitoring, and servicing of remotely operated vehicles (ROVs); shipboard oceanographic data processing and sample analysis; and precise navigation, trackline maneuvering, and station-keeping to support deep-ocean and coastal surveys. Expanding programs and continued support of other Federal agencies' survey missions may increase the use of NAVOCEANO ships in support of national priorities.

EPA operates two ships that monitor and assess impacts from ecological disturbances and ocean-based human activities on the ocean, Great Lakes, and coastal waters. EPA's Ocean Survey Vessel (OSV) *Bold* operates under the statutory requirement to monitor the deposition of dredged materials under the Marine Protection, Research, and Sanctuaries Act of 1972. This Act regulates intentional ocean disposal of materials and to authorize any related research, and also provides for the designation and regulation of marine sanctuaries. EPA's R/V *Lake Guardian* is operated by the Chicago-based Great Lakes National Program Office, which conducts monitoring programs that sample the water, aquatic life, sediments, and air in order to assess the health of the Great Lakes ecosystem.

NASA will continue to use ship time in support of calibration activities for satellite-based sensors; ocean biology, biogeochemistry, and ocean physics research; and validation of data products from space-based and aircraft-borne sensors. NASA investigators work collaboratively with other agencies to conduct oceanic research for approximately six months each year.

USGS foresees an increasing use of ships for seafloor and geophysical characterization related to habitat identification, establishment of continental shelf limits, and hazard assessment, particularly with respect to potential tsunami hazards. USGS technical capabilities will continue to be applied largely in collaboration with other Federal agencies in support of comprehensive environmental characterization. Not having its own ships, application of USGS expertise in data collection, analysis, and interpretation will be based on continued access to vessels of the Federal Oceanographic Fleet.

BOEM will continue to conduct deepwater research in the Gulf of Mexico Outer Continental Shelf region. In addition, with renewed interest in leasing and exploration of offshore oil and gas resources in the U.S. Arctic Ocean, a series of research projects in the Chukchi and Beaufort Seas have been developed in close coordination with interested Federal and public partners. The use of icebreakers and other support vessels to deploy and operate gliders, AUVs, or unmanned aircraft systems (UASs) in the Arctic Ocean will fill the data gaps and support future resource management decisions. Also of note, the Secretary of the Interior launched a "Smart from the Start" wind energy initiative for the Atlantic Outer Continental Shelf to facilitate sighting, leasing, and construction of new projects, spurring the rapid and responsible development of this abundant renewable resource. In support of this initiative, fleet capabilities may be relied upon to meet these data collection activities.

As the Federal agencies continue to plan and execute their program plans, adjustments in Fleet size and composition may be considered. For example; the NSF-funded Ocean Observing Initiative (OOI) designed to provide 25–30 years of sustained ocean measurements to study climate variability, ocean circulation, ecosystem dynamics, air-sea exchange, seafloor processes, and plate-scale geodynamics, is currently in the construction phase, and is expected to be operational in late 2014. The OOI will enable powerful new scientific approaches for exploring the complexities of Earth-ocean-atmosphere interactions, thereby accelerating progress toward the goal of understanding, predicting, and managing our ocean environment (*http://www.oceanobservatories.org*). Ships will be used to install, service, and remove oceanographic buoys, moorings, and deep seafloor infrastructure and instrumentation.

B. UTILIZATION

As defined for this *Federal Oceanographic Fleet Status Report*, capacity is the ability of the Fleet to support Federally funded projects in a timely and cost-effective manner. It is determined by considering a number of factors in combination: total operating budget, total number of ships in the Fleet (or in a particular class of ships in the Fleet); each ship's design, size, range, and endurance; total number of available science berths; ships' mission configurations; and the Fleet's geographic distribution. Fleet capacity impacts the number of operating days available, science-party size, maximum cruise lengths, and the ability to operate in certain areas.

For the purposes of Figure 1, agency vessels were combined into their respective classes to showcase the utilization trends over the past decade. The concept of total available operating days is the maximum operational tempo that can be sustained by the agency, withstanding budgetary constraints. The agency specific operational tempo is established based on required maintenance periods, sea trials and inspections, mission staging, and crew rest, leave, and training.

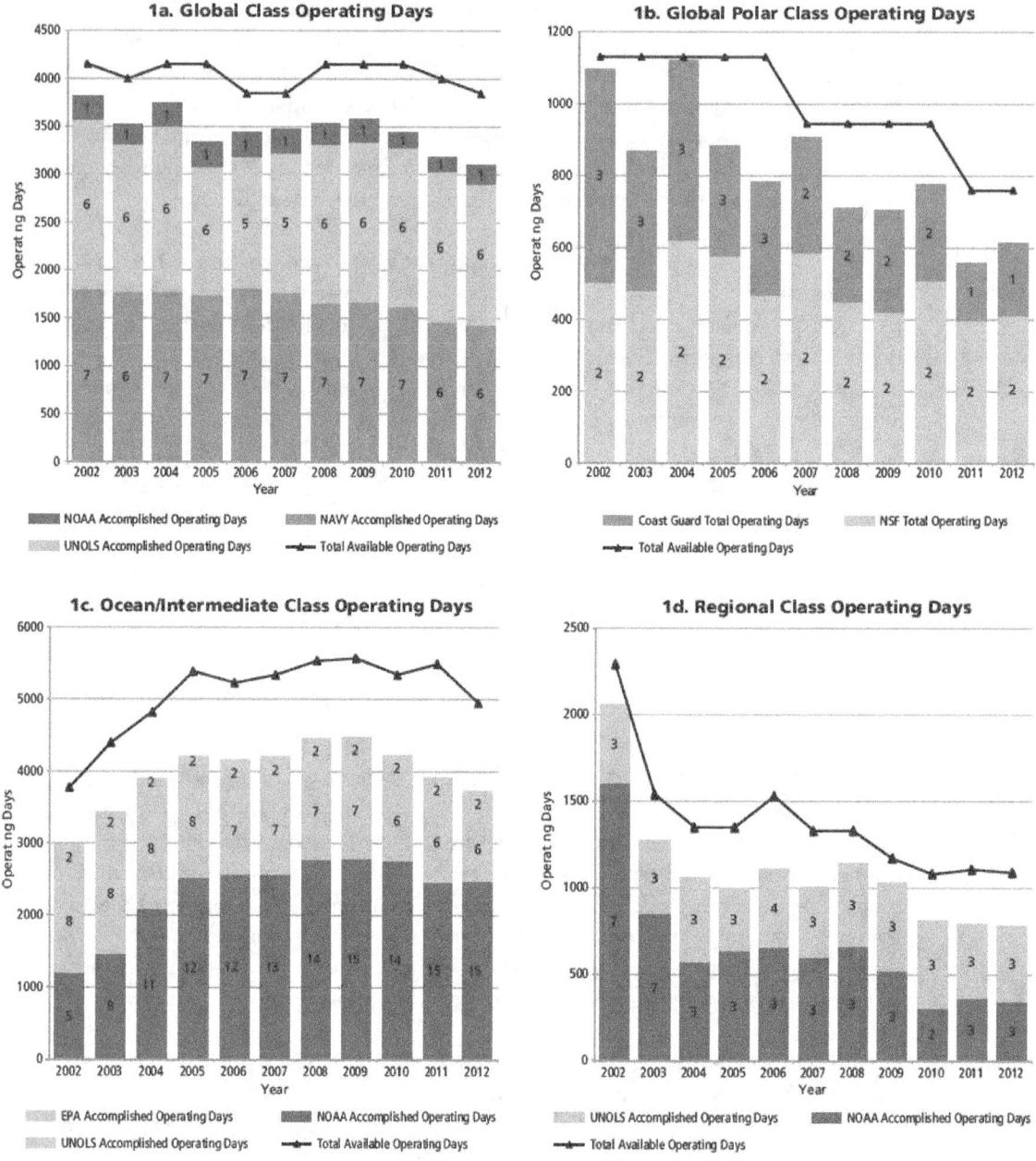

Figure 1. Fleet utilization by class for NOAA, EPA, NAVOCEANO, and UNOLS ships. Ship days include those used by all Federal agencies. The number inside each column represents the number of ships operated by each agency.

In an effort to continue operating at optimal tempos and more efficiently capitalize on vessels operating in specific geographic areas, the Fleet is focusing on strengthening existing Federal partnerships. For example, the USAP Polar Vessels have begun to support missions to include other NSF divisions (Ocean Sciences) and agencies (NOAA). The Fleet also supports NASA, BOEM, USGS, and USACE with their at sea requirements. NASA uses approximately four months of ship time each year to support their ocean research activities. BOEM continues to use UNOLS, NOAA, and chartered vessels to address their oceanographic needs. USGS and USACE also rely on the Fleet to support their mission needs.

Since 2002, the Fleet composition has experienced a dramatic shift across the classes. As the respective agency fleets have changed over the last decade, the overall availability continues to overshadow the accomplished operating days. In order to close the gap, agencies are taking a look at their fleet usage and composition.

By 2003, NOAA decommissioned four of their Regional Class vessels and replaced them with the more advanced Ocean Class vessels. Six of these were the former Navy Tactical Auxiliary General Ocean Surveillance (T-AGOS) with an average age of ten years. NOAA has also added four FSVs to their fleet of Ocean Class vessels.

In order to meet 2012 fiscal year (FY) budget demands, agencies were required to make difficult programmatic choices that ultimately resulted in changes to the Fleet. NOAA received approval to move forward with the disposal of the *Miller Freeman* and *Delaware II* and placed the *Ka`imimoana* and *McArthur II* in warm layup. NSF's demand for Intermediate Class ships has decreased due to increasingly complex missions and the inability to operate in high latitudes. Therefore, they continue to phase out this class with the retirement of the R/V *Wecoma* in 2012 and planned retirements of the Regional Class vessels R/V *Cape Hatteras* in 2013 and R/V *Point Sur* in 2014.

Overall, the decreasing trend in ship utilization rates is a result of several factors:

- A difficult budgetary environment
- Increased fuel costs (400% increase in price/gallon since 2003; see Figure 2)

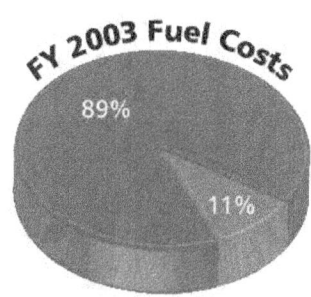

Fuel Costs: $13.88M
Operating Costs: $122.54M
Price/Gallon = $0.84

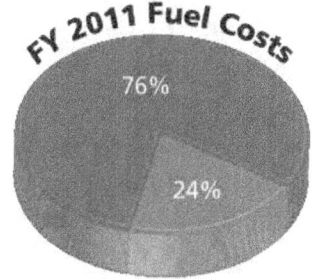

Fuel Costs: $44.36M
Operating Costs: $180.00M
Price/Gallon = $3.33

Figure 2. Total fuel costs for UNOLS, NOAA, and NSF Polar vessels represented 11% of total operating costs in FY2003 compared to 24% in FY2011. When fuel costs exceed the Office of Management and Budget's prescribed fuel rates, agencies are often required to choose between reducing operating days at sea or taking cuts to other programs.

- An aging fleet (average age = 23+ years) which ultimately results in higher maintenance costs and extended repair periods
- Increased personnel costs (e.g., salaries, mandatory training requirements, healthcare, etc.)
- An ever-increasing list of new safety and environmental operating standards for ship
- Decreased number of ship time requests within the academic fleet
- Increased post 9-11 port security requirements from U. S. Maritime Administration

Lengthy design and acquisition lead times (8-10 years) associated with ship renewals requires agencies to have recapitalization plans ready to address the projected ship capacity decreases beginning in 2020. The IWG-FI will continue to assess the Fleet capacity as existing programs change and new programs are funded.

C. CHALLENGES AND IMPACTS

The Federal agencies are facing numerous challenges associated with cost-effectively operating and maintaining the Fleet, while assessing the needs and plans for renewal of ships as they reach their projected end-of-service (EOS) life dates. EOS dates are flexible and reflect agency decision points based on current and predicted budgets, execution of maintenance plans, and emerging technologies. These challenges include matching fleet capabilities to agency missions, addressing rising operational costs, and meeting crew and training requirements. The Fleet often experiences times of high and low demand due to required ship specific capabilities, seasonal restrictions, or geographic limitations. Ships desired for one mission may be unavailable for another due to their technical specification for operation in high latitudes, acoustically quieted, or dynamic positioning capabilities. Agencies may face unexpected repair periods during the height of the field season while replacement parts for the older ships are no longer readily available. At times, the fleet is faced with cancelling, deferring or conducting missions in less than optimal circumstances. For example, missions can be scheduled onto alternative platforms that are more costly in an effort to complete the project within the timeline required.

The IWG-FI is strongly supportive of Federal agency missions and continues to work together to address these challenges. In the wake of rising costs, the IWG-FI is working to coordinate operational and maintenance plans for the ships in the Fleet as a way to increase support for agency missions. Despite best efforts, when Federal managers are faced with budget shortfalls as a result of rising costs, the options available to them are few. Agencies are forced to take funds from core science programs (if available); switch to sub-optimal modes of operation, including additional sharing of ships between agencies beyond efficient levels; seek additional opportunities to conduct research or survey work that is funded from other non-Federal sources; reduce research and operations plans; defer research and maintenance; and schedule nonoperational periods and/or retire ships. Although these actions may resolve short-term funding problems, they perpetuate funding and scheduling issues in the out years and limit the ability of scientists to conduct valuable research, education, and survey activities.

Ship operators are also challenged in hiring qualified crew, especially engineers, due to increased training requirements. Agencies cannot afford to provide the full scope of training needed to qualify crew for higher level licenses. In addition to the licensing requirements; the sea going challenges and lifestyle, and competition from the commercial shipping industry are affecting the ship operators' ability to retain and recruit qualified marine technicians and crew. The IWG-FI is working to address the challenges of operating and maintaining the Fleet in the face of rising costs, while also assessing and planning for renewal, as needed, to ensure the appropriate level of Fleet capacity will be available in the future.

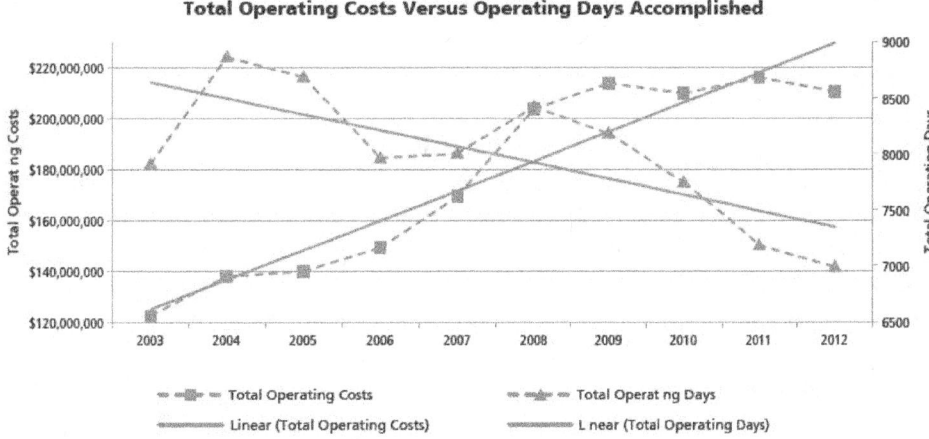

Total Operating Costs Versus Operating Days Accomplished

Figure 3. Total operating costs for UNOLS, NOAA, and NSF polar vessels have increased dramatically over the past five years. Costs for FY12 are estimates. The costs of operating ships have increased dramatically, but Federal agency budgets have not kept pace, resulting in fewer operating days accomplished. The Federal agencies are reviewing all options for mitigating increased Fleet costs, including scheduling nonoperational periods and/or retiring ships.

NOAA

4. FLEET RENEWAL AND MODERNIZATION

A. 2012-2035: RESEARCH SHIPS

Currently there are 12 Global Class, 11 Ocean Class (four of which are the older Intermediate Class ships), and three Regional Class research ships. Seven of these research ships are expected to remain in service beyond 2025 (Figure 4). As of this writing, three funded (appropriated) ships (*Sikuliaq*, AGOR-27, and AGOR-28) should enter the fleet between 2013 and 2015 (Figure 5). The two Ocean Class ships appropriated by Navy (AGOR-27 and AGOR-28) and the three Regional Class ships (RCRV 1–3) being studied by NSF would support transition of the Fleet from the technologically obsolete Intermediate Class to a capable and properly capitalized research Fleet for accomplishing U.S. research objectives in ocean science for the next three decades.

GLOBAL CLASS

Twelve Global Class ships, six of which are multipurpose oceanographic research vessels, support U.S. science objectives at sea (Figure 4). The NOAA Ship *Ronald H. Brown* and three Navy vessels—*Thomas G. Thompson, Roger Revelle,* and *Atlantis*—are between 15 and 21 years old. Two Navy vessels—*Melville* and *Knorr*—will be retired in 2014 after 45 years of service. NOAA plans a mid-life refit project for the *Ronald H. Brown* by 2015. ONR is identifying requirements for a mid-life refit and service life extension program for the *Thomas G. Thompson*, *Revelle*, and *Atlantis*, potentially extending the service life of the three ships to 40 years, which will significantly increase the overall Federal Oceanographic Fleet Global Class research capacity out to 2030.

Research Fleet

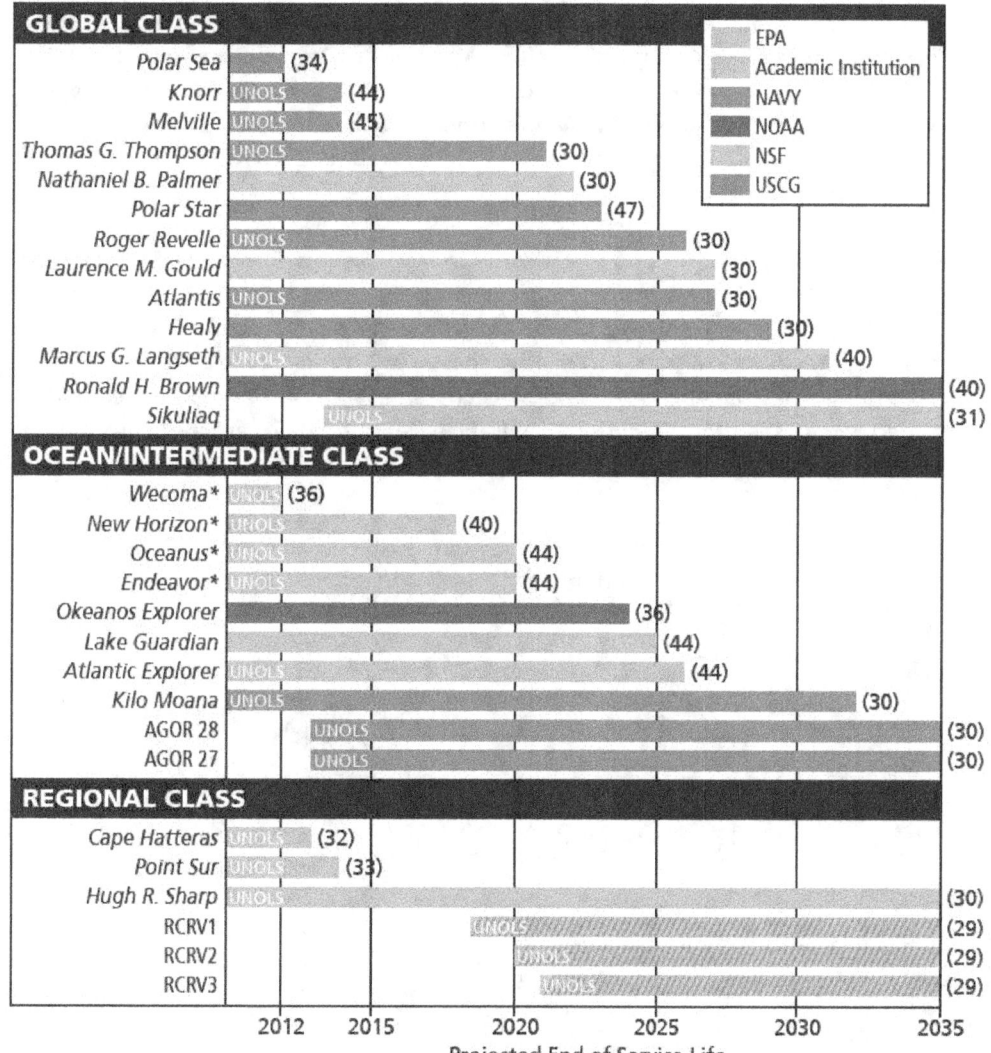

*Represent the older, less-capable Intermediate Class vessels that will be replaced by Ocean Class vessels.

Figure 4. *Projected End of Service life dates by Class for research vessels currently in the Fleet or with a projected date of delivery. Numbers in parentheses provide the age of the vessel at projected end of service life. Note: The Laurence M. Gould and Nathaniel B. Palmer are both under long-term lease by NSF and represent the Nation's entire capacity to support Antarctic research. RCRV1/2/3 are currently undergoing design study from FY2012 appropriations.*

The U.S. polar fleet is currently composed of five ice-capable, Global Class vessels. Three are icebreakers operated by the U.S. Coast Guard: the medium icebreaker *Healy* and the two heavy icebreakers *Polar Sea* and *Polar Star*. Currently, only the *Healy* is operational. NSF's OPP holds long-term leases for two other vessels: the light Research Vessel Icebreaker *Nathaniel B. Palmer* and the ice-reinforced Antarctic Research and Supply Vessel *Laurence M. Gould*. These two vessels have been continuously in service with the USAP for 20 years (*Nathaniel B. Palmer*) and 14 years (*Laurence M. Gould*). Preliminary discussions are underway for a *Nathaniel B. Palmer* replacement vessel, to be delivered by its projected end of service life in 2022 (see Figure 4). A sixth vessel, NSF's new ice-reinforced R/V *Sikuliaq*, is currently under construction and scheduled for delivery in mid-2013 and entry into the Fleet for funded science work in the Arctic planned for mid-2014.

One Global Class research ship specialized for deep-ocean drilling, *JOIDES Resolution*, began operations in 1978 as an oil exploration vessel, but was converted for scientific research in 1985 when the ship was leased from Overseas Drilling Limited to support the Ocean Drilling Program (ODP). The rig can drill to an ocean depth of 8,235 m (27,018 ft). In 2003, the ODP concluded and the lease for the *JOIDES Resolution* ended when scientific drilling activities were finished. NSF entered into a lease agreement again with Overseas Drilling Limited where the *JOIDES Resolution* will

Federal Oceanographic Fleet Modernization (2007–2015)

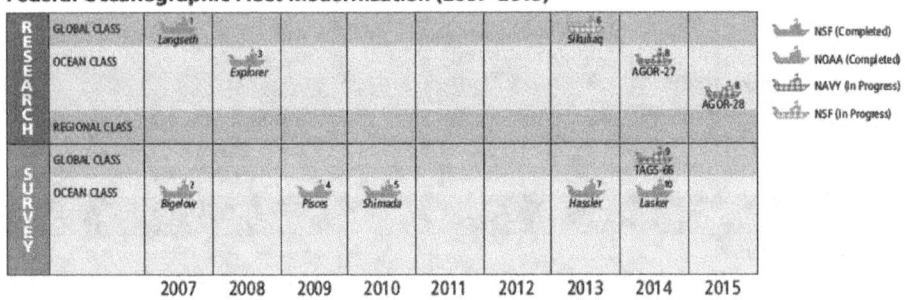

¹NSF completed *Marcus G. Langseth* acquisition/conversion from FY 2004–2006 appropriations.
²NOAA completed *Henry B. Bigelow* acquisition/construction from FY 2007 President's Budget Request for operating funds.
³NOAA completed *Okeanos Explorer* acquisition/conversion from FY 2005 appropriations.
⁴NOAA completed *Pisces* acquisition/construction from FY 2005 appropriations.
⁵NOAA completed *Bell M. Shimada* acquisition/construction from FY 2006 appropriations.
⁶NSF *Sikuliaq* acquisition/construction (on-going) from FY 2007–2009 appropriations for construction funds through NSF MREFC account.
⁷NOAA completed *Ferdinand R. Hassler* acquisition/construction from FY 2007–2009.
⁸Navy AGOR 27 & 28 acquisition/construction (on-going) from FY 2008 President's Budget Request for Navy ship construction.
⁹Navy TAGS-66 acquisition/construction (on-going) from FY 2007 appropriations.
¹⁰NOAA *Reuben Lasker* completed acquisition/construction from FY 2009 ARRA funds.

NOTE: NSF RCRV-1/2/3 undergoing design study from FY 2012 appropriations.

Figure 5. Fleet renewal and modernization by agency, class, and function, as described in this Fleet Status Report. Ship icons are located on the year in which they are anticipated to enter the Federal Oceanographic Fleet. The solid color ships highlight the agencies' ability to successfully plan and execute their respective renewal plans that were reflected in the 2007 Fleet Status Report.

operate in support of the IODP that was initiated in 2004. One Global Class research ship specializes in two-and three-dimensional multichannel seismic research, NSF's *Marcus G. Langseth*, which entered service in 2007 and is expected to support research operations through 2030.

OCEAN CLASS

There are eight Ocean Class research ships, four of which will be at or beyond their projected EOS dates by 2020 (Figure 4). It is important to note that although categorized here as Ocean Class vessels, three of the older NSF ships were designated as Intermediate Class in the 2001 and 2007 Fleet Status Reports, and are significantly smaller and less capable than the Ocean Class ships being considered as replacements. Of these vessels, NSF retired R/V *Wecoma* in 2012. R/Vs *Endeavor* and *Oceanus* will be 45 years old at their projected retirement in 2020. Scripps-UCSD R/V *New Horizon* will reach its projected EOS life in 2018. The *Atlantic Explorer* operated by the Bermuda Institute of Ocean Sciences will reach its projected EOS life in 2026.

The ONR-owned R/V *Kilo Moana* entered the Fleet in 2002 and is expected to be in service until 2032. The Navy appropriated funds in FY11 and FY12 for the construction of two Ocean Class ships (AGOR-27 and -28 in Figure 5). These new ships represent an important transition of the Fleet research capacity to modern, technologically advanced ships capable of meeting the scientific research missions of the Nation for the next 30 years.

NOAA's only Ocean Class research vessel, *Okeanos Explorer,* entered the Federal Oceanographic Fleet in 2008, and supports ocean exploration.

EPA's *Lake Guardian* is expected to remain in service until at least 2025.

REGIONAL CLASS

R/V *Cape Hatteras* will be retired in 2013 and R/V *Point Sur* in 2014 (Figure 4). NSF is studying the design for three new Regional Class research ships to support the Fleet modernization efforts. The main operating areas covered by these new ships would be the East Coast, West Coast, and Gulf of Mexico. There would be open competitions for a UNOLS institution to manage the design and construction process, as well as for operators of each of these new ships. The University of Delaware's R/V *Hugh R. Sharp*, which entered service in 2005, is a modern, technologically advanced research vessel with acoustic quieting, dynamic positioning, advanced equipment handling systems, and multiple sonar capabilities to support current and expected research requirements for the next 25 years.

B. 2012-2035: SURVEY SHIPS

Currently, there are six Global Class, 15 Ocean Class, and three Regional Class survey ships (Figure 6). The majority of the Ocean and Regional Class ships are specialized to support fisheries and hydrographic survey work. The Global Class vessels conduct Department of Defense survey operations.

GLOBAL CLASS

The Navy owns the six active Global Class survey vessels, all of which are less than 20 years old. The Navy's newest vessel, TAGS-66, is expected to be operational in 2014.

OCEAN CLASS

There are 15 Ocean Class survey vessels that are further classified as Fisheries or Survey. NOAA owns and operates all but one, which EPA owns. The FSVs are specialized to conduct fisheries stock assessment surveys, marine resource management, and marine mammal surveys. NOAA's *Fairweather, Rainier*, and *Thomas Jefferson* conduct hydrographic surveys to produce accurate nautical charts required for safe navigation, national security, and maritime commerce. The remaining vessels are involved with marine ecosystem monitoring and environmental data collection.

NOAA's Ocean Class research vessels *McArthur II* and *Ka`imimoana* were placed in a warm layup status in 2012 as a result of budget constraints. By 2022, all NOAA T-AGOS vessels will exceed thirty years of active service. EPA's only survey vessel, OSV *Bold*, is expected to be transferred or disposed of in 2013. NOAA Ship *Miller Freeman* is scheduled for decommissioning in early 2013. NOAA's newest FSV, *Reuben Lasker*, was launched in 2012 and it is anticipated to be operational in 2014.

REGIONAL CLASS

NOAA has three Regional Class survey vessels. NOAA Ship *Ferdinand Hassler* supports hydrographic survey and *Oregon II* supports fisheries survey. NOAA Ship *Delaware II* supported fisheries survey and was decommissioned in 2012.

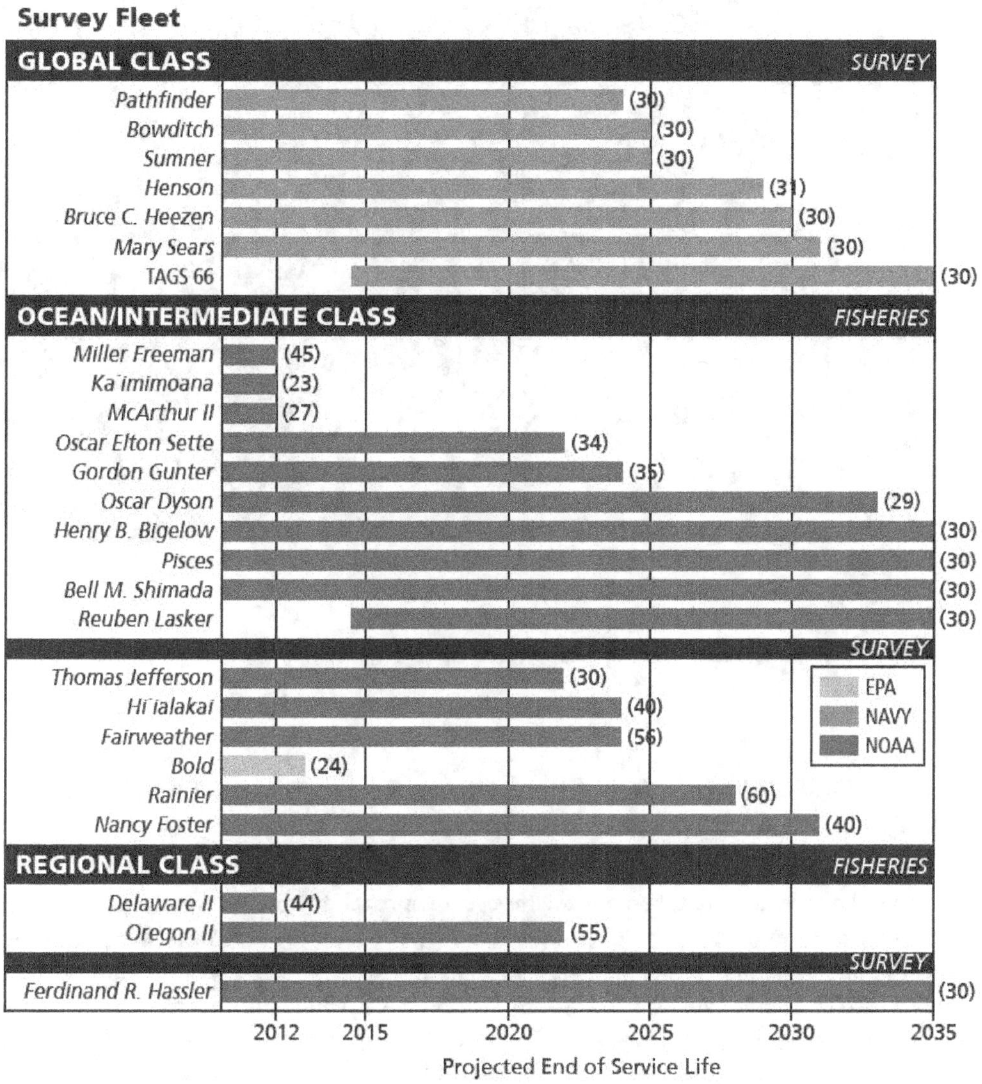

Survey Fleet

Figure 6. Projected end of service life dates by Class for survey vessels currently in the fleet or with a projected date of delivery. Numbers in parentheses provide the age of the vessel at projected End of Service Life.

5. PLANNING CONSIDERATIONS

A. LIFE CYCLE COSTS:
PLANNING CONSIDERATIONS, DESIGN, ACQUISITION, MAINTENANCE, AND DISPOSAL

Federal agencies have taken a total life-cycle approach to the Federal Oceanographic Fleet from design through disposal (Figure 7). Of particular note is the lead time required for design and acquisition in planning for ship renewals. Oceanographic research and survey vessels are expected to complete a 30-year service life for the ship hull, with regularly scheduled maintenance and upgrades of onboard electronics, hotel services, and quality-of-life systems. Although design and acquisition planning is based on the service-life expectancy, technology advancements have provided opportunities to extend the service life of many of the larger ships beyond 30 years. These decisions require careful evaluation of the impact on total ownership costs.

As with all forms of capital equipment, the final stage of a ship's life-cycle management is associated with disposal options and costs. Unlike less-complex systems, ship disposal may have long-term berthing, salvaging, scuttling, and environmental implications. Although each ship is different, there are many common disposal considerations. Depending on the condition of the vessel and equipment, there is the possibility of transfer to another agency, academic institution, or foreign nation. Lessons learned have been shared by the Federal agencies through the IWG-FI to ensure disposal is done safely and with the greatest possible return or the least possible cost.

B. TECHNOLOGY INFUSION

In the future, there will be increasing opportunities to incorporate modernized ship design concepts and technology trends in mechanical engineering, information technology, acoustic quieting, and sea-keeping into new construction, conversions, and upgrade projects. In addition, new sensors and data collection platforms such as ROVs and gliders will augment ships' capabilities, and will require reassessment of the most efficient and effective infrastructure needed to support a given mission.

Capitalizing on the studies done cooperatively by IWG-FI agencies on common hull configurations, acoustically quiet ship designs, and advanced over-the-side handling systems, NSF is proceeding with design plans and intends to fund construction of three new highly capable, technologically advanced Regional Class ships. NOAA intends to evaluate the Regional Class design for survey operations to potentially economize on the design cost for the next phase of the *NOAA Ship Recapitalization Plan* (NOAA, 2008).

Nominal Ship Acquisition and Life-Cycle Timeline

	YR1				YR2				YR3				YR4				YR 5		YR 6		YR 7		YR 8		YR 9–37	
	Q1	Q2	Q3	Q4	Q1	Q2	Q3	Q4	Q1	Q2	Q3	Q4	Q1	Q2	Q3	Q4											
PRE-PHASE 1																											
Requirements Definition																											
Concept Explorat on																											
Develop Preliminary Statement of Requirements																											
Develop Acquis t on Strategy																											
PHASE 1: Preliminary/Contract Design																											
F nalize Statement of Requirements																											
Develop and Issue Operator RFP																											
Select Operator						▲																					
Develop and Issue Industry Team RFP																											
Develop Design and Proposal																											
Select Compet tive Design											▲																
PHASE 2: Detailed Design and Construction																											
Detailed Design																											
Cr t cal Des gn Review														▲													
Construct Sh p 1																											
Trials/Delivery/Post-Shakedown Availability																											
PHASE 3: Operations																											
Ship 1																											
Disposal																										▲	

Figure 7. Conceptual Ocean Class service life time line. Procurement of large research vessels requires many years to develop a design, acquire funding, negotiate and award the contract, and build and deliver the ship.

Innovative technologies in the maritime industry are shaping the conduct of Federal Fleet operations and their posturing for the future. For instance, the Federal Oceanographic Fleet can now obtain small, ship-launched UASs. Additionally, benthic profiling gliders show promise as observational platforms that could reduce the number of buoy tending missions currently handled by the Fleet. AUV technologies have progressed in navigational accuracy, mission duration, and observational capabilities. It is expected that in 2013 the Navy and NOAA will conduct the first AUV bathymetric surveys meeting International Hydrographic Organization standards.

Multimission operational modes are currently being explored. NOAA has conducted ship-launched small UASs in the northern Pacific on the *Oscar Dyson* and the *McArthur II*, paving the way for future technology infusion for marine mammal surveys and other Earth observation missions. The recently launched NOAA Ship *Ferdinand R. Hassler* is a Small Waterplane Area Twin Hull (SWATH) vessel. The SWATH design provides improved stability and sea-keeping, permitting hydrographic operations to continue in inclement weather that would have curtailed traditional mono-hull vessels.

Construction over the last five years has enabled NOAA to expand to five FSVs that employ active and passive hull quieting technologies for conducting fisheries assessments. The Navy is constructing two new Ocean Class vessels with planned delivery by the end of 2015. In 2014, NSF will field the new Global Class R/V *Sikuliaq* that is capable of working in and around first-year ice, providing the scientific community with broader access to the Arctic Ocean. New construction of Regional and Ocean Class vessels and the life-extension of Global Class ships will introduce advanced technologies to the Federal Oceanographic Fleet, increasing effectiveness and efficiency.

Beyond the hardware designs of ships and associated unmanned systems, technological improvements in software and communications have enabled tremendous gains in data distribution and sensor control. For instance, NOAA Ship *Okeanos Explorer* conducts systematic telepresence-enabled ocean exploration in unknown and poorly understood regions. The ship can stream up to three HD video feeds and data from 4000 m depth-capable ROVs, and mapping and sensor systems. Scientists at shore-based Exploration Command Centers can view the real-time video and data and interact with onboard scientists and technicians and other scientists around the world. Data, products, and metadata move quickly from research and survey ships to shore through the "rolling deck to repository" in six weeks or less, ensuring broad public access. Streaming live over the Internet into newsrooms, science centers, classrooms and living rooms engages audiences in the excitement of ocean exploration and increases ocean literacy.

C. OTHER OPPORTUNITIES

Ships of the Federal Oceanographic Fleet are designed for the specific needs of each agency (Appendix 2); however, most ships are capable of supporting work outside their primary mission. Opportunities for cross-agency use of the Fleet are coordinated and scheduled through UNOLS or directly between agencies through Interagency Agreements and Memoranda of Agreement. Federal agencies also charter commercial vessels and use private sector ship support, when appropriate, to accomplish missions such as environmental monitoring, buoy servicing, icebreaking, and bathymetric mapping.

NOAA contracts commercial vessels to supplement its core capabilities, recognizing the increased capacity brought to bear on hydrographic surveying, the better the agency can support safe navigation in U.S. waters. In 2012, NOAA had seven firms under contract to provide hydrographic surveying services. The number of hydrographic surveys conducted by contract depends on appropriations, and they typically are about half of the total hydrographic data collection effort. NOAA's strong partnerships with the private sector and academia have fostered technology improvements as well as process improvements for hydrographic surveying.

NSF also contracts commercial vessels. These ships provide mission-critical fuel, cargo, and heavy icebreaker support for the annual resupply of McMurdo Station, Antarctica. Occasionally, these vessels support scientific research in addition to their primary resupply or icebreaking missions.

D. POLAR

NSF and USCG currently support U.S. polar research. NSF's OPP funds and manages the U.S. Antarctic Program (USAP), which supports scientific research, environmental stewardship, and maintains a geopolitical presence in Antarctica and the Southern Ocean as mandated by Presidential Memorandum 6646 and Presidential Decision Directive NSC-26. For the past 20 and 14 years, respectively, Antarctic research has been conducted aboard RVIB *Nathaniel B. Palmer* and ARSV *Laurence M. Gould*, while the annual break-in of McMurdo Sound has until 2007 been performed by a USCG heavy icebreaker. Beginning in 2008, the USAP has contracted icebreaker services with various foreign nations and companies (Sweden, IB *Oden*; Russian Federation, IB *Krasin*; Murmansk Shipping Company, IB *Vladimir Ignatyuk*), retaining USCGC *Polar Sea* as a standby icebreaker in Seattle until her engines failed in June 2010[1]. While these stopgap measures have enabled Antarctic research to continue, it is unclear that Swedish and Russian icebreakers will be available in the future.

National Security Presidential Directive (NSPD) 66/Homeland Security Presidential Directive (HSPD) 25 of 9 January 2009 states that the United States is an Arctic nation and establishes that the policy of the United States in the Arctic includes

NSF

Reports by the National Research Council (NRC, 2011b), the White House Office of Science and Technology Policy (Augustine et al., 2012), and Members of Congress[2] stipulate that the United States should provide heavy icebreakers to support U.S. interests at both poles. For example, Future Science Opportunities in the Antarctica and Southern Ocean (NRC, 2011b) identifies the continued strong logistical support of Antarctic science, specifically calling out the need to "maintain and enhance the unique logistical assets of the United States, including...research vessels with increased icebreaking capabilities, and heavy icebreakers for reliable resupply of the U.S. Antarctic Program." More and Better Science in Antarctica Through Increased Logistical Effectiveness (Augustine et al., 2012) specifically called out the need to "Restore the U.S. polar ocean fleet (icebreakers, polar research vessels, mid-sized and smaller vessels) to support science, logistics, and national security in both polar regions over the long term. (Follow through on pending action in the President's FY2013 Budget Request for USCG to initiate the design of a new icebreaker.)" The report included as one of its actions items (Action 4.1-3): "Aggressively pursue the acquisition of a new polar research vessel with enhanced capabilities to ensure U.S. leadership in pursuing scientific endeavors in the Southern Ocean."

1 USCGC Polar Sea is inactive, awaiting determination of disposition; crew, critical parts and funding were transferred to USCGC Polar Star to complete her reactivation work and ready her for mission execution, currently anticipated in late 2013

2 http://www.cantwell.senate.gov/public/index.cfm/2012/6/cantwell-begich-murkowski-announce-plan-to-halt-scrapping-of-key-icebreaker

scientific monitoring and research into local, regional, and global environmental issues and investigation of the Extended Continental Shelf and Boundary issues.

Since 2001, Arctic research has primarily been performed aboard USCGC *Healy* through funding by NSF. R/V *Sikuliaq* is expected to significantly augment research in this important region.

E. GREEN INITIATIVES

The Federal Oceanographic Fleet is currently implementing several changes to improve fuel efficiency, reduce pollution, and decrease the carbon footprint of its ships. These upgrades will help mitigate the environmental impacts of the Fleet as well as reduce operating costs through heightened efficiency and reduced operating costs.

Decreasing fuel consumption and engine emissions are two primary objectives of IWG-FI agencies. Several improvements are in place while many others are currently under development. EPA, NOAA, and the Navy are using ultra low-sulfur diesel, which significantly reduces harmful air emissions. The engines of R/V *Lake Guardian* and R/V *Sikuliaq* were outfitted with EPA tier 2 upgrades which reduce harmful emissions. NOAA is planning similar upgrades for its ships. Biodiesel and other alternative fuels will comprise an increasing portion of fuel usage on Federal vessels; the Navy aims to use 50% of alternative fuels by 2020 in its survey ships. NOAA Ship *Bell M. Shimada* is using some biodiesel and NOAA's Great Lakes Environmental Research Laboratory (GLERL) vessels (R/Vs *Huron Explorer*, *Shenehon*, and *Laurentian*) operate entirely on soy-based diesel. The Navy is currently installing hybrid electric drives on its ships and future fuel-efficiency projects include fuel cells and friction drag reduction. The Navy is also in the process of equipping its ships with navigation aids that are projected to reduce fuel costs by 4–8%. NOAA is also installing fuel management and monitoring systems throughout the Fleet to provide real-time displays of fuel consumption from the ship's engines to the bridge and engine room. Ship operators use this information (i.e., gallons/nautical mile, gallons consumed/engine, electrical power generated) to optimize fuel demands in order to operate more efficiently and maximize fuel savings. These ongoing efficiency measures will reduce the Federal Oceanographic Fleet's reliance on fossil fuels and reduce operating costs in the face of rising fuel costs.

In addition to reducing fuel usage, both NOAA and the Navy are reducing onboard energy consumption through initiatives such as the installation of solid-state lighting, which uses 10% of the electricity of traditional lighting and reduces mercury waste.

The Navy has also added low-solar absorption coatings on the ship decks. Several IWG-FI agencies are raising energy awareness through installation of energy dashboards, electric meters, energy audits, and better fuel metering.

EPA uses low-toxicity hull coatings and nontoxic fire-fighting foam on its ships. EPA ballast water management limits potential transfer of invasive species between different water bodies. The NOAA GLERL vessels as well as the NOAA Ships *Okeanos Explorer* and *Bell M. Shimada*, and the NSF R/V *Sikuliaq*, have replaced lubricants and oils with biodegradable, petroleum-free products. R/V *Sikuliaq* and the NOAA FSVs also limit underwater noise pollution.

IWG-FI agencies are dedicated to reducing the environmental impacts of the Federal Oceanographic Fleet. NOAA publishes a quarterly green fleet newsletter that continues to raise awareness and highlight the greening efforts of the agency. NOAA also requires shipboard environmental compliance officer training to ensure that these environmental measures are followed.

NOAA

6. VISION—THE FUTURE FEDERAL OCEANOGRAPHIC FLEET

Beyond the currently funded endeavors outlined in Section 4, Federal agencies are in various stages of engaging stakeholders in the development of long-term strategies and plans requiring oceanographic vessels for research or surveying purposes.

NATIONAL SCIENCE FOUNDATION

The USAP, which is managed and funded by NSF's OPP, currently provides researchers with the ice-reinforced ARSV *Laurence M. Gould,* and the light icebreaking RVIB *Nathaniel B. Palmer.* Both vessels, under long-term lease to NSF, have been actively engaged in Antarctic research support continuously since 1998 and 1992, respectively. As these vessels approach their 30-year life span (2022 for the *Palmer,* 2028 for the *Gould),* OPP has worked to determine the capabilities and requirements for the next generation of polar-capable research vessels.

Through workshops (Leventer et al., 2002, UNOLS PRV SMR Refresh Committee, 2012) involving hundreds of scientific, technical, and research vessel experts from academic institutions, other Federal agencies (USCG, NOAA, Navy), and foreign polar institutions (Sweden, Germany), as well as numerous reports over the last decade, the scientific and technical requirements of a new, advanced Polar Research Vessel (PRV) have continued to be refined.

NATIONAL OCEANIC AND ATMOSPHERIC ADMINISTRATION

As a follow on to the *NOAA Ship Recapitalization Plan* (NOAA, 2008), the NOAA Fleet Composition: 2012–2027 (NOAA Fleet Composition) focuses on how the NOAA fleet should evolve over the next 15 years. That evolution will be shaped by examining the types of data that NOAA needs to acquire to serve the Nation, and also the most efficient ways to use a mix of Federal and non-Federal ships, small vessels, and unmanned platforms to meet those observational needs, including implementing emerging technologies into NOAA operations. The NOAA Fleet Composition will also help inform vessel size, number of ships required to meet NOAA's mission, and timing for future shipbuilding plans.

The NOAA Fleet Composition includes input from partners in the Federal Oceanographic Fleet to ensure that the NOAA fleet is built to support Federal programs. NOAA's at sea research and survey requirements will continue to be evaluated along with the technologies available to meet them in order to identify the most cost-effective solutions and ensure the NOAA fleet can continue to meet the Nation's science and environmental stewardship needs for many years to come.

UNITED STATES NAVY

At present, the Navy has not programmed funds for building future Global Class survey vessels to replace its current fleet. However, to ensure that mission requirements and Fleet capabilities will best serve the Nation, the Navy plans to include in their FY15–FY17 Program Objective Memorandum, Research, Development, Test, and Evaluation, funding to conduct research and develop preliminary designs for the potential next generation of ocean survey vessels. The research will help inform vessel size, number of ships required to meet the Navy's mission, and timing for future shipbuilding plans. The Navy's current fleet of oceanographic survey vessels was constructed between 1994 and 2001. Consequently, based on a 30-year service life expectancy, the Navy will not have to start replacing its fleet until 2024. Due to long design and acquisition lead times involved with replacing ships, the Navy will initiate the process in 2015 to avoid potential gaps in surveying capability.

ENVIRONMENTAL PROTECTION AGENCY

EPA has no programmed funding directed specifically to shipbuilding or conversion. Additionally, there is no single program for ship management. The two EPA vessels are managed independently, OSV *Bold* out of EPA Headquarters, and R/V *Lake Guardian* out of the Chicago regional office. R/V *Lake Guardian* has secure funding for current and near future operations. Due to increasing operating costs, EPA is in the process of transferring or disposing of OSV *Bold*, and expects to cease ownership and operations of the ship in FY13. The assessment for OSV *Bold* considers multiple path scenarios including transfer or disposal of the vessel, potential shared funding partnerships, and continuing operations with reduced mission capability.

UNITED STATES COAST GUARD

The FY13 budget request for USCG includes resources in FY13 to begin a new polar icebreaker acquisition project. In 2013, USCG will develop operational requirements with its Federal agency partners to acquire an icebreaker of the right capability to support missions traditionally conducted by Federal partners with polar region interests.

7. CONCLUSIONS

Although there has been an increase in the use of satellites, floats, gliders, and scientific seafloor cabled observatories, ships are fundamental tools needed to advance our knowledge of the ocean and are critical components of ocean survey/research infrastructure. They make it possible to acquire the data necessary to understand the complex Earth system, more carefully manage ocean resources for the benefit of society, and respond to catastrophic events around the globe.

This *Federal Oceanographic Fleet Status Report* describes the current capacity and capabilities to support the Nation's vital interests in understanding the world ocean. The currently programmed and appropriated Global, Ocean, and Regional Class ships will maintain overall Fleet capacity through 2020 (Figure 8). Future Fleet capacity needed to support projected national ocean priorities through 2035 will be determined by individual agency requirements and coordinated through the IWG-FI in order to assess opportunities to increase the overall efficiency and effectiveness of the Federal Oceanographic Fleet.

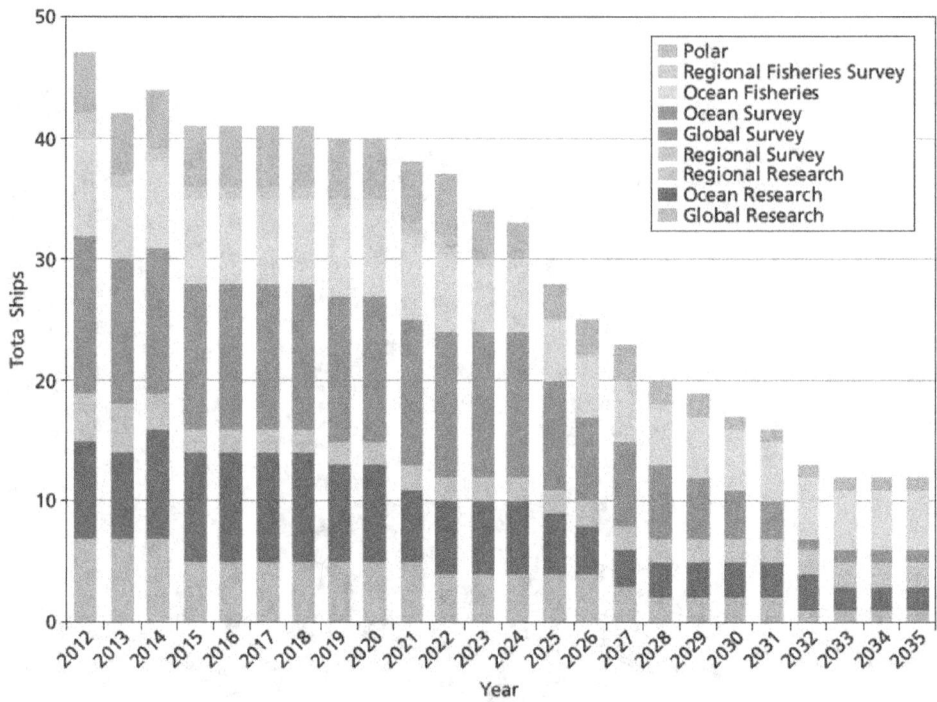

Figure 8. *The existing ships along with those modernization efforts identified in Figure 5 will enable the Fleet capacity to remain stable through 2020. Without further fleet modernization, the Federal Oceanographic Fleet will experience a 50% decline by 2026.*

8. REFERENCES

Augustine, N.R., T. Allen, C.E. Dorman, H.W. Ducklow, B. Gordon, R.K. Harrison, D. Hartill, G. Jugie, L.J. Lanserotti, D.J. McNabb, R. Spearing, and D.H. Wall. 2012. *More and Better Science in Antarctica through Increased Logistical Effectiveness, Report of the U.S. Antarctic Program Blue Ribbon Panel.* Study conducted at the request of the White House Office of Science and Technology Policy and the National Science Foundation, Washington, D.C., 224 pp. Available at: *http://www.nsf.gov/od/opp/usap_special_review/usap_brp/rpt/index.jsp.*

Levanter, A., J. Anderson, J. Ardai, L. Bartek, S. Borg, S. Brachfeld, S. Cande, G. Christeson, E. Domack, J. Holik, S. Ishman, T. Janacek, et al. 2002. *Antarctic Marine Geology and Geophysics Planning Workshop Final Report.* Washington, D.C., 15 pp. Available at: *http://www.usap.gov/usapgov/vessel/ScienceAndOperations/contentHandler.cfm?id=409.*

National Oceanic and Atmospheric Administration (NOAA). 2008. *NOAA Ship Recapitalization Plan.* 144 pp. Available at: *http://www.omao.noaa.gov/publications/08_ship_recap_plan.pdf.*

National Oceanic and Atmospheric Administration. 2010. *Chart the Future: NOAA's Next Generation Strategic Plan Executive Summary.* National Oceanic and Atmospheric Administration, Office of Program Planning and Integration, Silver Spring, MD, 24 pp. Available at: *http://www.ppi.noaa.gov/wp-content/uploads/NGSP_ExecSumm.pdf.*

National Research Council (NRC). 2009. *Science at Sea: Meeting Future Oceanographic Goals with a Robust Academic Research Fleet.* The National Academies Press, Washington, D.C., 120 pp.

National Research Council. 2011a. *Critical Infrastructure for Ocean Research and Societal Needs in 2030.* The National Academies Press, Washington, D.C., 98 pp.

National Research Council. 2011b. *Future Science Opportunities in the Antarctica and Southern Ocean.* The National Academies Press, Washington, D.C., 230 pp.

NST Joint Subcommittee on Ocean Science and Technology. 2007. *Charting the Course for Ocean Science in the United States for the Next Decade: An Ocean Research Priorities Plan and Implementation Strategy.* Washington, D.C., 84 pp. Available at: *http://www.whitehouse.gov/sites/default/files/microsites/ostp/nstc-orppis.pdf.*

UNOLS PRV SMR Refresh Committee. 2012. *A New U.S. Polar Research Vessel (PRV): Science Drivers and Vessel Requirements.* Final Report, 38 pp. Available at: *http://www.unols.org/committees/fic/smr/PRV.*

U.S. Commission on Ocean Policy (USCOP). 2004. *An Ocean Blueprint for the 21st Century.* Final Report, Washington, D.C., 36 pp. Available at: *http://www.oceancommission.gov/documents/full_color_rpt/welcome.html.*

APPENDIX 1.
SHIPS IN THE FEDERAL OCEANOGRAPHIC FLEET >130 FEET

OWNER	CLASS	PURPOSE	NAME	LENGTH (ft)	DATE OF DELIVERY	PROJECTED END OF SERVICE[1]	AGE AS OF 2012	AGE AT EOS
NOAA	Ocean	FS	Miller Freeman	216	1967	2012	45	45
NOAA	Regional	FS	Oregon II	170	1967	2022	45	55
NOAA	Regional	FS	Delaware II	171	1968	2012	44	44
NOAA	Ocean	FS	Oscar Elton Sette	224	1988	2022	24	34
NOAA	Ocean	FS	Gordon Gunter ·	224	1989	2024	23	35
NOAA	Ocean	FS	Oscar Dyson	208	2004	2035	8	31
NOAA	Ocean	FS	Henry B. Bigelow	209	2005	2036	7	31
NOAA	Ocean	FS	Pisces	209	2007	2038	5	31
NOAA	Ocean	FS	Bell M. Shimada	209	2010	2040	2	30
NOAA	Ocean	FS	Reuben Lasker	209	2014	2044	N/A	30
NAVY (U[2])	Global	MPR	Melville	279	1969	2014	43	45
NAVY (U[2])	Global	MPR	Knorr	279	1970	2014	42	44
NSF (U[2])	Ocean	MPR	Endeavor	184	1976	2020	36	44
NSF (U[2])	Ocean	MPR	Oceanus	184	1976	2020	36	44
NSF (U[2])	Ocean	MPR	Wecoma	185	1976	2012	36	36
SIO (U)	Ocean	MPR	New Horizon	170	1978	2018	34	40
EPA	Ocean	MPR	Lake Guardian	168	1981	2025	31	44
NSF (U[2])	Regional	MPR	Cape Hatteras	135	1981	2013	31	32
NSF (U[2])	Regional	MPR	Point Sur	135	1981	2014	31	33
BIOS(U[2])	Ocean	MPR	Atlantic Explorer	168	1982	2026	30	44
NOAA	Ocean	MPS	McArthur II	224	1985	2012	27	27
NOAA	Ocean	MPR	Okeanos Explorer	224	1988	2024	24	36
NOAA	Ocean	MPS	Ka'imimoana	224	1989	2012	23	23
NAVY (U[2])	Global	MPR	Thomas G. Thompson	274	1991	2021	21	30
NSF (U[2])	Global	MPR	Marcus G. Langseth	235	1991	2031	21	40
NAVY (U[2])	Global	MPR	Roger Revelle	274	1996	2026	16	30
NAVY (U[2])	Global	MPR	Atlantis	274	1997	2027	15	30
NOAA	Global	MPR	Ronald H. Brown	274	1997	2037	15	40
NAVY (U[2])	Ocean	MPR	Kilo Moana	186	2002	2032	10	30
UD (U[2])	Regional	MPR	Hugh R. Sharp	146	2005	2035	7	30
NSF (U[2])	Regional	MPR	RCRV1[5]	175	2019	2048	N/A	29
NSF (U[2])	Regional	MPR	RCRV2[5]	175	2020	2049	N/A	29
NSF (U[2])	Regional	MPR	RCRV3[5]	175	2021	2050	N/A	29
NOAA	Ocean	MPS	Rainier	231	1968	2028	44	60
NOAA	Ocean	MPS	Fairweather	231	1968	2024	44	56
NOAA	Ocean	MPS	Hi'ialakai	224	1984	2024	28	40
EPA	Ocean	MPS	Bold	224	1989	2013	23	24
NOAA	Ocean	MPS	Nancy Foster	187	1991	2031	21	40
NOAA	Ocean	MPS	Thomas Jefferson	208	1992	2027	20	35
NAVY	Global	MPS	Pathfinder	328	1994	2024	18	30
NAVY	Global	MPS	Sumner	328	1995	2025	17	30
NAVY	Global	MPS	Bowditch	328	1995	2025	17	30
NAVY	Global	MPS	Henson	328	1998	2029	14	31
NAVY	Global	MPS	Bruce C. Heezen	328	2000	2030	12	30
NAVY	Global	MPS	Mary Sears	328	2001	2031	11	30
NOAA	Regional	MPS	Ferdinand R. Hassler	137	2009	2040	3	31
NAVY	Global	MPS	TAGS 66	328	2014	2044	N/A	30
NAVY (U[2])	Ocean	MPR	AGOR 27	235	2014	2044	N/A	30
NAVY (U[2])	Ocean	MPR	AGOR 28	235	2014	2044	N/A	30
USCG	Global	Polar	Polar Star[4]	399	1976	2023	36	47
USCG	Global	Polar	Polar Sea	399	1978	2012	34	34
USCG	Global	Polar	Healy	420	1999	2029	13	30
NSF (U[2])	Global	Polar	Sikuliaq	261	2013	2044	N/A	31
NSF	Global	Polar	Nathaniel B. Palmer[3]	308	1992	2022	20	30
NSF	Global	Polar	Laurence M. Gould[3]	230	1997	2027	15	30

[1] Projected End of Service dates are based on Operator estimates; typically these are a 30-year service life or 15-years after a mid-life refit. When a vessel reaches its projected 'End of Service' date, this will trigger a decision point for the Operator to: 1) Re-invest in the vessel; 2) Place vessel in inactive status; 3) De-commission/Transfer Vessel

[2] University National Oceanographic Laboratory System (UNOLS) is a coordinating body for the national academic research fleet.

[3] Leases for the *Laurence M. Gould* and the *Nathaniel B. Palmer* were renewed in 2010 and 2012, respectively for five years with an additional five one-year options.

[4] When *Polar Star*'s reactivation is complete in 2013, USCG expects the service life to be extended 10 years

[5] RCRV 1/2/3 are currently undergoing a design study

FS: Fisheries Survey
MPR: Multipurpose Research
MPS: Multipurpose Survey

APPENDIX 2.
RESEARCH AND SURVEY ACTIVITIES BY AGENCY

	ONR	NAVOCEANO	NOAA	NSF	EPA	BOEM	NASA	USCG	USGS
Science and Technology (Research)									
Earth System Sciences	U/P		U/P	U/P	U/P	U	U		U
Exploration			U/P	U/P			U		
Living Marine Resources	U/P		U/P	U/P	U/P				U
Polar	U		U/P	U/P			U	P	
Observation Systems Development	U/P			U/P					

	ONR	NAVOCEANO	NOAA	NSF	EPA	BOEM	NASA	USCG	USGS
Resource Management									
Hydrographic Surveys	U/P	P	U/P	U/P	U/P	U	U	P	U
Bathymetric Surveys	U/P	P	U/P	P	U/P	U		P	U
Living Marine Resources Surveys			U/P	U/P	U/P	U			U
Geophysical Surveys				U/P					U
Polar		.	U/P	U/P			U	P	U
Observation Systems Support	U/P		U/P	U/P			U	P	

	ONR	NAVOCEANO	NOAA	NSF	EPA	BOEM	NASA	USCG	USGS
Education and Outreach			P	U/P	P	U	U	P	

P= Provides ship/vessel time U= Uses ship/vessel time

APPENDIX 3.
ACRONYMS AND ABBREVIATIONS

AUV . . . . Autonomous Underwater Vehicle
BIOS . . . . Bermuda Institute of Ocean Sciences
BOEM . . . . . . Bureau of Ocean Energy Management
DARPA . . . . . . Defense Advanced Research Projects Agency
DoE . . . . Department of Energy
EPA . . . . Environmental Protection Agency
FS . . . . Fisheries Survey
FSV . . . . Fisheries Survey Vessel
FY . . . . Fiscal Year
GLERL . . . . . . Great Lakes Environmental Research Laboratory
HOV . . . . Human Occupied Vehicle
ICES . . . . International Council for the Exploration of the Seas
IODP . . . . . . Integrated Ocean Drilling Program
IOOS . . . . . . Integrated Ocean Observing System
IWG-FI . . . . . . Interagency Working Group on Facilities & Infrastructure
JOIDES . . . . . . Joint Oceanographic Institutions for Deep Earth Sampling
MPR . . . . Multi-Purpose Research
MPRSA . . . . . . Marine Protection, Research and Sanctuaries Act of 1972
MPS . . . . Multi-Purpose Survey
MREFC . . . . . . Major Research Equipment and Facilities Construction
NASA . . . . . . National Aeronautics and Space Administration
NAVOCEANO . . . Naval Oceanographic Office
NM . . . . Nautical Miles
NOAA . . . . . . National Oceanic and Atmospheric Administration
NSC . . . . National Security Council
NSF . . . . National Science Foundation
PRV . . . . Polar Research Vessel
ODP . . . . Ocean Drilling Program
ONR . . . . Office of Naval Research
OOI . . . . Ocean Observatories Initiative
OPP . . . . Office of Polar Programs
OSTP . . . . . . White House Office of Science Technology Policy
OSV . . . . Ocean Survey Vessel
RCRV . . . . . . Regional Class Research Vessel
R/V . . . . Research Vessel
ROV . . . . Remotely Operated Vehicle
SODV . . . . . . Scientific Ocean Drilling Vessel
SOST . . . . . . Subcommittee on Ocean Science and Technology
SWATH . . . . . Small Waterplane Area Twin Hull
T-AGOS . . . . . Tactical Auxiliary General Ocean Surveillance
USACE . . . . . . United States Army Corps of Engineers
USAP . . . . . . United States Antarctic Program
USCG . . . . . . United States Coast Guard
UNOLS . . . . . . University National Oceanographic Laboratory System

Special thanks to the National Oceanographic Partnership Program Office for providing significant report support, and to Jason Mallett of the Consortium for Ocean Leadership for report design. Additional editing and design services were provided by Ellen Kappel and Johanna Adams of Geosciences Professional Services Inc.

MAY 2013